"For many years I have been on a quest to draw near to God, who seemed distant and illusive to me. Much to my surprise, He condescended and met me as I took Linda's challenge to seek Him daily in worship. As I slowly bowed my hopes and dreams before the Lord, I was dazzled by His love and filled with awe and delightful expectation."

— BEV DESALVO, pastor's wife from Texas

"*Satisfy My Thirsty Soul* is the beautiful depiction of the lifelong pursuit of true intimacy with Christ. Linda Dillow's words and soul-provoking study questions made their way into my life and left me thirsting for nothing more than more of Him."

— KATHY CORDELL, Cheyenne, Wyoming

"*Satisfy My Thirsty Soul* has opened a doorway to worship that is transforming my drab, daily life from "the grind" to His Glory. I will read (and need) this book again and again."

— SANDI FUNKHAUSER, Boise, Idaho

FOR I AM DESPERATE FOR
YOUR PRESENCE

Satisfy My Thirsty *Soul*

LINDA DILLOW

NAVPRESS

Discipleship Inside Out®

NAVPRESS
Discipleship Inside Out®

NavPress is the publishing ministry of The Navigators, an international Christian organization and leader in personal spiritual development. NavPress is committed to helping people grow spiritually and enjoy lives of meaning and hope through personal and group resources that are biblically rooted, culturally relevant, and highly practical.

For a free catalog go to www.NavPress.com
or call 1.800.366.7788 in the United States or 1.800.839.4769 in Canada.

ISBN-13: 978-1-57683-390-2

Cover Design: studiogearbox.com
Cover Illustrator: Allen Garns
Creative Team: Liz Heaney, Darla Hightower, Arvid Wallen, Kathy Guist

Some of the anecdotal illustrations in this book are true to life and are included with the permission of the persons involved. All other illustrations are composites of real situations, and any resemblance to people living or dead is coincidental.

Unless otherwise identified, all Scripture quotations in this publication are taken from the New American Standard Bible (NASB), © The Lockman Foundation 1960, 1962, 1963, 1968, 1971, 1972, 1973, 1975, 1977, 1995. Other versions used include: THE MESSAGE (MSG). Copyright © 1993, 1994, 1995, 1996, 2000, 2001, 2002, 2005. Used by permission of NavPress Publishing Group; the Amplified New Testament (AMP), © The Lockman Foundation 1954, 1958; the HOLY BIBLE: NEW INTERNATIONAL VERSION® (NIV®), Copyright © 1973, 1978, 1984 by International Bible Society, used by permission of Zondervan Publishing House, all rights reserved; the Holy Bible, New Living Translation (NLT), copyright © 1996, 2000. Used by permission of Tyndale House Publishers, Inc., Wheaton, Illinois 60189. All rights reserved; and the King James Version (KJV).

Dillow, Linda.
  Satisfy my thirsty soul : for I am desperate for Your presence / Linda Dillow.
      p. cm.
  Includes bibliographical references (p.   ).
  ISBN 978-1-57683-390-2
  1. Christian women--Religious life. 2. Spiritual life--Christianity.
3. Worship. I. Title.
BV4527.D55 2007
248.8'43--dc22
                                        2007004620

Printed in the United States of America
8 9 10 11 12 13 14 / 17 16 15 14 13

To my Beloved,
Thank you for drawing me into deep, private worship and into your
presence. This book is my offering to you.

Contents

ACKNOWLEDGMENTS   9

PART 1: WAKING UP TO WORSHIP

1. MY THIRSTY SOUL   13

2. MY WORSHIP AWAKENING   31

3. MY SOUL FINDS STILLNESS   49

4. EXPANDING MY WORSHIP EXPERIENCE   69

PART 2: WALKING IN WORSHIP

5. I BOW MY LIFE   89

6. I BOW MY WORDS   107

7. I BOW MY ATTITUDE   125

8. I BOW MY WORK   143

9. I BOW MY TIMES OF WAITING   161

10. I BOW MY PAIN   181

11. I BOW MY WILL   203

12. DRAWN INTO HIS PRESENCE   223

TWELVE-WEEK BIBLE STUDY   243

NOTES   295

ABOUT THE AUTHOR   303

acknowledgments

A special thanks to

My wonderful husband, Jody. Thank you for teaching me how to study God's Word.

My special friend, Lorraine Pintus. Thank you for your expert counsel and editing. You have walked through every page with me.

My "super editor," Liz Heaney. Thank you for your excellent skills as an editor and your encouragement as a friend.

The wonderful team at NavPress. Special thanks to Kent Wilson, Kris Wallen, and Darla Hightower. It is a priviledge to work with you!

Many thanks to the dear women who were in the pilot Bible study: Darlene Kordic, Judy Dunagan, Valerie Cox, Chee-Hwa Tan, and Jodi Nunn. And thanks too to the three women who took the Bible study over the Internet: Bev De Salvo, Kathy Cordell, and Sandi Funkhauser.

Part 1

Waking Up to Worship

Chapter 1

—

My
Thirsty
Soul

My Thirsty Soul

O God, you are my God,

earnestly I seek you;

my soul thirsts for you,

my body longs for you,

in a dry and weary land

where there is no water.

PSALM 63:1, NIV

The setting was ideal for a twenty-first century fairy tale. Hidden away from the main road in a quaint Austrian village, the four-hundred-year-old church stood next to a farmhouse with window boxes filled with geraniums. Wheat stalks swayed in the fields and cows lowed in the barn, creating an intoxicating old-world charm.

I was in this delightful setting for a family celebration, the marriage of my son Nicolai to his beloved, Christina. The wedding ceremony would take place here, in this picture-perfect stone church, and the dinner and reception would be in a castle. Definitely fairy tale material.

As I sat in the first row of the church, I looked behind me at Christina, who was waiting to come down the aisle. Such exquisite joy illumined her face that I gasped out loud. Then I gazed at my son, waiting at the front of the sanctuary for his bride. He was taking such delight in her that his face shown as if a neon light blinked inside him.

Of course, I cried as the bride came face-to-face with her bridegroom. I watched my son drink her in with his eyes as she proclaimed, "I love you so much, Nic!" They were oblivious of their audience, oblivious of the flickering candles casting a glow on their faces. Only the two of them existed. Their faces expressed the sentiment of their hearts: "We have found what we were looking for."

Don't all women hope to feel this same way? Don't our hearts clamor for deep soul satisfaction, for a oneness that quenches our thirst for closeness and satisfies our empty places?

I've talked to thousands of women, and no matter what language we speak or what country we call home, most of us yearn for face-to-face intimacy. Some describe intimacy as *into-me-see*. Many women seek to find such intimacy through marriage.

I certainly did. I was twenty-one years old and a new Christian when I married Jody. Having spent my teenage years flitting like a butterfly from one boyfriend to the next, I made a vow to my new Lord that went something like this: *God, I'm through with guys. I'm going to be like my mentor and stay single and travel around the country and speak.* Nice vow, but two weeks after I made it, I spotted Jody Dillow across the room at a Christian conference for college students and *plotted* to meet him. We were married a year later.

I married young because I found a great man. I married young because I was thirsty for intimacy and deep love. Having grown up with an abusive, alcoholic father, I had holes in my heart. Now I had Jesus and Jody, and was I excited! Jesus gave me purpose in life, and Jody . . . oh, I was excited to be his bride! Visions of deep communication, soul connection, and intimate, joyous lovemaking danced in my head. I was going to be the Wife of the Century. We would have an intimate oneness that was breathtaking and all-encompassing. Each year our intimacy would grow ever deeper.

After four children and forty-three years of marriage, I can say that Jody and I have grown more in love with each other. Our intimacy has deepened, along with our respect and acceptance of each other. But that doesn't mean that our marriage has been easy. While a few years were almost fairy-tale-like, others have been far from a fairy tale. Deep intimacy always requires work, acceptance, and forgiveness. Lots of it.

Women begin marriage with the expectation of deepening intimacy, but, sadly, in most marriages intimacy fades. Children, jobs, house payments, and a hectic life erode the longed-for intimacy, substituting it with daily drudgery.

No woman I know got married in order to be a cook and housekeeper to a man, but too often a wife settles for serving her husband. Oh yes, she loves him and he loves her, but who has time for breathtaking oneness when children need to be bathed, dinner prepared, and the lawn mowed?

Women also search for intimacy in our relationships with other women. Friendship, fun, food, laughter, and trust. But many experience only surface friendships about clothes, kids, and food, when what we hope for is to find a dear friend with whom we can share our hearts.

I wanted face-to-face friendships with women, but wondered, *Is this even possible?* At age fifty I moved from Austria to Hong Kong and began making new friends. When I was fifty-three, God made it clear to Jody and me that we were to move back to the States, and feelings of loneliness filled my heart. I cried, "No, God, I can't start all over again with friendships. It takes too long when you don't have a history together." But God had a surprise waiting for me in Colorado Springs — my soul sister, my writing and speaking partner, Lorraine Pintus. We know each other's hearts; we feel each other's pain. We even finish each other's sentences!

Once when Lorraine and I were on stage at an Intimate Issues Conference (based on one of the books we have coauthored, *Intimate Issues*), she told the audience, "It is really great to travel with Linda because being with Linda is like being with nobody!" I had to assure the surprised audience that her words were *really* a compliment! Lorraine was trying to communicate that such a oneness characterizes our friendship that we are free to talk or be silent, free to drop to our knees to pray and worship, free to be who we are.

Yes, I longed for deep intimacy in marriage and for authentic *into-me-see* friendships with other women. But most of all, I yearned for intimate knowing in my relationship with Christ. As a new believer I often said my purpose was to know Him and make Him known. Too often, though, my emphasis was on *making Him known* rather than on *knowing Him*. I had been purposeless before becoming a Christian, and now I had a purpose: Win the world for Christ. My heart was adorned with service and ministry. To be sure, it was a noble goal, but often this pursuit superseded loving my Lord and sitting at His feet and worshipping Him.

I longed for intimacy, ecstasy, and a deep relationship with my Bridegroom, but as the years passed and life became hectic and complicated, I settled for serving the One I loved. My loving Bridegroom walked the earth, searching, calling, bending down, and tenderly whispering to my heart in hopes of slowing me down long enough to embrace Him. He gently called to me:

"Linda, will you come sit on my lap?"

Lord, I have to prepare a Bible study. I'll come later . . .

"Linda, will you come talk with me?"

Lord, I have to cook a meal for some of your children. I promise I'll come later.

But "later" never came. I was just too busy doing good things *for* Him.

My desire to serve God was good, but my priorities were out of order. God's Word clearly says that the *first* and most important thing is this: to love God with all our being (see Matthew 22:37-38). This is the first and greatest commandment. The *second* commandment is loving others, which includes ministry or works of service (see Matthew 22:39). I had reversed these two commandments.

It's so important to be able to say, *I am not primarily a worker for God; I am first and foremost a lover of God. This is who I am.* "All of us need to be lovers who work rather than workers who love."[1] But I was a worker who loved. The result was overload and burnout.

When our priorities become turned around, and we place more emphasis on loving others than on loving God, we are headed for spiritual and physical exhaustion. This is where I was in 1994. I called out to God, *Satisfy my thirsty soul, for I am desperate for your presence! Oh, God, restore the joy of my salvation!*

SEARCHING FOR SOMETHING MORE

I remember well one day in 1994. I sat on my navy blue couch in the living room of my fifth-floor Hong Kong apartment, watching a gecko skitter across the wall. As I looked out my window at myriad high-rise apartment buildings, I felt stirrings and longings I didn't understand. Why did I feel so empty? I loved my husband and my family. I loved the Lord. What more could any woman want? I was a faithful servant of my God, willing to move from continent to continent to teach and train women. I had everything that should bring soul satisfaction, yet deep down, where no one but God sees, I was thirsty for more. But what was the "more"?

And why was I thirsty? Because I was bone-weary from being on the mission field for many years. I was thirsty because I wanted more of God. I longed for a personal encounter with Him. God spoke to me in His Word, but I desired to hear His personal voice to me. I yearned for joy unspeakable, for a deeper union and oneness, for spiritual, bridal union. I didn't want to settle for God's omnipresence, where I knew He was everywhere, or even for His wonderful, abiding presence. I thirsted for a face-to-face intimacy with God.

I was crying out to Him. I wasn't sure what I was crying out for, and I didn't know where it would take me, but I knew I would never experience face-to-face intimacy with God until I put Him first and service second. I can't tell you why I couldn't see that intimate knowing of God must come before serving Him. I only know that God began to woo me, to place within me a desire to know Him intimately.

WHAT GOD LONGS FOR

I began reading through the Bible, looking for passages about intimacy, and soon found evidence that God seeks intimacy with each of us, including you and me. Scripture describes our relationship with Him with word pictures of love, marriage, sexuality, and fidelity. Here are some examples:

God loves us with an everlasting love. He loved us first (see Jeremiah 31:3).

He calls Himself the Bridegroom and He calls us the bride (see 2 Corinthians 11:2).

God calls idolatry "adultery" (Isaiah 57:7, NLT).

He says that we are to be as close to Him spiritually as we are physically to our husbands in our sexual union: "For this reason a man shall leave his father and mother and shall be joined to his wife, and the two shall become one flesh. This mystery is great; but I am speaking with reference to Christ and the church" (Ephesians 5:31-32).

I first understood the holy beauty in these verses when Lorraine Pintus and I wrote *Intimate Issues*. The Lord allowed me to see that He chose the closest, most intimate act on earth, the sexual union between husband and wife, to portray the holy beauty of my spiritual intimacy with Him. It was as if He said, "Look, Linda, and understand. Enter into the glorious joy of the marriage union. See, feel, and deeply know physical intimacy and ecstasy. Then lift your eyes, my daughter — lift them and know — this is the degree of spiritual intimacy and ecstasy that I long to share with you."

As I studied the Word, I became convinced that God seeks intimacy with us. I also saw that face-to-face intimacy with God is a choice.

The Choice of Face-to-Face Intimacy

In both the Old and New Testaments we see four levels of intimacy with God. We see it in the relationship that the Israelites had with God, and we also see it in the relationship that Jesus' followers had with Him.[2]

As we look at the levels of intimacy the Israelites had with God, envision a bull's-eye with four circles, with the outer circle representing a flagging interest in God and the inner circle — the bull's-eye — representing face-to-face intimacy.

The general Israelite population represents *the outer circle*, which is the largest group and the furthest away from God. God was about to give Moses the Ten Commandments, and He asked Moses to prepare all the people for the manifestation of His presence on Mt. Sinai. They would see God's visible presence, but they were forbidden to come near Him. Boundaries were set to ensure that the people did not come up the mountain (see Exodus 19:11-12).

The priests and elders represent *the second circle* of intimacy, which is closer to God. Moses and the elders of Israel pressed past the barriers and had a much more intimate vision of God than the people had. They must have felt the presence of God. They experienced far more than the general population, but seeing a vision of God did not change their lives. Only a short time later, they were worshipping the golden calf (see Exodus 24:9-11).

Moses and Joshua represent *the third circle,* which is yet closer to God. Joshua often lingered in God's presence (see Exodus 33:11). He longed to be where God manifested Himself. Joshua

ascended higher on the mountain of glory than any other, except
Moses (see Exodus 24:13-14).

Moses represents *the inner circle,* which is face-to-face intimacy.
He talked face-to-face with God as a friend. Remarkable! After
God brought the Israelites out of Egypt, Moses led them to Mt.
Sinai. On several occasions God summoned Moses to climb the
mountain and fellowship with Him. Twice intimate encounters
lasted for forty days. "Thus the LORD used to speak to Moses face
to face, just as a man speaks to his friend" (Exodus 33:11). This is
true intimacy—friend-to-friend, face-to-face. When the glory of
the Lord settled on Mt. Sinai, Moses alone communed with God
(Exodus 24:15-17).

Just as the Old Testament pictures four levels of intimacy
between the Israelites and God, the Gospels show us four levels
of intimacy between Jesus and His disciples. Again, envision
the bull's-eye with the goal, face-to-face intimacy, as the center.
Jesus chose *seventy* men and then sent them out two-by-two (the
outer circle). Jesus chose *twelve* disciples to be His inner group (the
second circle). *Three* of those disciples shared greater intimacy with
Jesus: Peter, James, and John (the third circle). *One* disciple called
himself "the disciple whom Jesus loved" (the inner circle). During
the Last Supper, John rested against Jesus' breast, a posture of
deep intimacy.

Both Moses and John chose intimacy. Moses said, "Let me
know Your ways" (Exodus 33:13). I think that what he was asking
was, "Take me deeper into your confidence, God." John chose to
nestle up to Jesus' breast. Any of the disciples could have experienced this intimate relationship with Jesus, but only John chose it.
Intimacy is a choice. We either do the work required to keep the
fire alive, or we don't.

As I continued searching God's Word, I realized that Paul,
David, and Mary—who all knew God intimately—chose the one
important thing.

THE MOST IMPORTANT THING

Paul's salvation experience on the road to Damascus had taken place about thirty years before he wrote these words about desiring "one thing." He wrote: "But *one thing* I do: forgetting what lies behind and reaching forward to what lies ahead, I press on toward the goal for the prize of the upward call of God in Christ Jesus" (Philippians 3:13-14, italics mine). Paul had won many spiritual battles and had grown much in those years. But he still had more spiritual heights to climb.[3] Paul wanted the first century believers to know that his "one thing" was to run toward God and press in to Him.

David also chose to passionately pursue "one thing." He wrote: "*One thing* I have asked from the LORD, that I shall seek: that I may dwell in the house of the LORD all the days of my life, to behold the beauty of the LORD and to meditate in His temple" (Psalm 27:4, italics mine).

In *Pleasures Evermore*, author Sam Storms observes:

> David desired to dwell in the presence of God, to behold God, to meditate upon the beauty and splendor of God, to bask in the invigorating light and glory of everything that makes God an object of our affection and delight and adoration.... The results of this passionate pursuit of God are staggering. Not only is beholding the beauty of the Lord indescribably enjoyable, it is profoundly transforming.[4]

We become like the one we think about, the one we gaze upon. Both Paul and David were transformed as they beheld the beauty of the Lord. This is because "beholding is a way of becoming."[5] As we behold Christ, we are changed. Transformed. As we meditate on the beauty and character of Christ, some of His goodness rubs off on us.

When Mary of Bethany's sister, Martha, complained that Mary was not helping her prepare the meal for Jesus and His disciples, Jesus replied: "Martha, Martha, you are worried and bothered about so many things; but only *one thing* is necessary, for Mary has chosen the good part, which shall not be taken away from her" (Luke 10:41-42, italics mine). Jesus did not say Martha's service was unimportant; He pointed out that Mary's choice to sit at His feet to learn and worship Him was the best choice. His words to Martha were His words to me. He said Martha had reversed the order of worship and service.

Paul's *one thing* was David's *one thing* was Mary's *one thing*. As I realized these truths, I faced a big question: Would I also choose face-to-face intimacy with God? Would my pursuit of Him become my one thing? Yes! None of this being at the foot of the mountain for me! I longed to be a woman of *one thing*: face-to-face intimacy with my God.

When I shared my desire with a friend, she said, "Linda, isn't that a bit presumptuous? To know the Creator of the universe intimately? To talk with Him face-to-face?" I did not think it was presumptuous. I believed it was biblical, so I prayed, *God, I want to intimately know you, wherever it takes me, whatever the cost.*

I wanted to know: How in the world do I become like Moses, John, Mary, David, and Paul? What is the path to this face-to-face intimacy, and how do I find it? God used a friend and His Word to answer my questions.

MY PATH TO GOD'S PRESENCE

Those who know the Lord intimately often make us painfully hungry for a deeper experience of Christ. It is the greatest of all influences — to provoke another to thirst, to pant as a deer after the Living Water.

Over eleven years ago, I visited Mimi Wilson's home for the

first time. We shared a delicious lunch, as Mimi is a renowned cook. Right after the delightful meal, she said, "Let's worship together." I thought, *I wonder what we're going to do.* Mimi turned on some worship music and fell to her knees. Having no clue what was to come, I followed her example and knelt by her couch. We basked in a sweet silence as the music played softly. We whispered words of honor, declaring the wonder and majesty of the Father, and for the first time I had an inkling of what it meant to "worship the LORD in the beauty of holiness" (Psalm 29:2, KJV). Time stood still and prayer flowed naturally from our worship. When I got up off my knees, I knew I had been enveloped by the presence of God. This was par for the course for Mimi. Through her, I learned that I too could bask in the presence of God.

Had I experienced an emotional state, or does God say we can experience His presence? I went to the Word to see for myself. I wanted evidence. Here is what I uncovered.

First, Psalm 89 says that in the act of worship, God can become a reality to us. "Happy are those who hear the joyful call to worship, for they will walk in the light of your presence, LORD" (verse 15, NLT).

This is what C. S. Lewis discovered. The famous author of *The Chronicles of Narnia* struggled with God's desire to be adored and praised. He couldn't understand why God wanted to be the center of affection and attention. But then Lewis understood that "in the process of being worshipped . . . God communicates His presence to men."[6]

Second, Psalm 63 goes even further, teaching us that worship can satisfy our thirsty souls. David wrote:

> O God, you are my God,
>   earnestly I seek you;
> my soul thirsts for you,
>   my body longs for you,

in a dry and weary land
    where there is no water.
I have seen you in the sanctuary,
    and beheld your power and your glory.
Because your love is better than life,
    my lips will glorify you. (verses 1-3, NIV)

The Message captures David's excitement:

God — you're my God!
    I can't get enough of you!
I've worked up such hunger and thirst for God,
    traveling across dry and weary deserts.

So here I am in the place of worship, eyes open,
    drinking in your strength and glory.
In your generous love I am really living at last!

God's presence so overtakes David as he worships that he says he will bless the Lord with every breath.

Third, in Psalm 16, David says soul satisfaction comes from knowing God's presence.

You will make known to me the path of life; in
Your presence is fullness of joy; in Your right
hand there are pleasures forever. (Psalm 16:11)

Think about what David is saying. God wants to give us a joy that infinitely transcends all other joys combined in the power and potential to satisfy, thrill, fill, and fulfill us. He offers us spiritual ecstasy, which is incomparable, unparalleled, and unfathomable. And He says it will be found in only one place: in His presence, at His right hand.[7]

As I studied the Word and witnessed others who were

experiencing deep emotional intimacy with God through private worship, this truth became clear: *Worship is the path to experiencing the presence of God, the way to face-to-face intimacy.*

THE FACETS OF WORSHIP

Worship? Are you confused? "What," you ask, "does worship have to do with my thirsty soul being satisfied?" Perhaps your idea about worship is similar to Mindy's, a woman I met at a retreat. I was speaking on becoming a woman of purpose, contentment, faith, and worship. Mindy's comment to me was this: "Linda, I was excited to come to this retreat because I want to be a woman of purpose, contentment, and faith, but I couldn't figure out why you were speaking about worship. Singing just isn't my thing." To Mindy, worship was simply singing praise songs.

I can remember when I felt like Mindy. I used to believe that worship was the twenty minutes of corporate singing before the sermon on Sunday morning. But I was so wrong! Worship is a multifaceted diamond.

I wanted to learn all there was to know about worship, so I began reading through the Bible, from Genesis to Revelation, and asked God to teach me. I must be a slow learner because this is the seventh year that I've read through the Bible, and my request is still the same. During these years, God has led me to a startling discovery:

> *Worship is not just a specific act. It is also a lifestyle.*
> *Worship is a specific act of bowing my knees and declaring, "Holy, holy, holy."*
> *Worship is also a lifestyle of bowing my life and living "holy, holy, holy."*

Worship begins in holy expectancy and ends in holy obedience. The specific act of worship—bowing my knees in holy expectancy—has taken me into the presence of God and true intimacy. The lifestyle of worship — bowing my life in holy obedi-ence — has taken me to a new level of living faithfully for Christ.

Here is what these two aspects of worship look like in my life. In the morning when I kneel in worship before the Lover of my soul, I worship Him with my words, with song, and in the beauty of stillness and silence. I praise Him with the Psalms of David and with personal psalms that flow from my heart of love. I listen for His voice. Then I get up and walk in the world of relationships with a husband, grown children, grandchildren, and friends.

As I walk through my life, I walk differently than I did before I began to understand what worship looks like. Now, I see all my life as an opportunity to bow before my King in worship. I can worship as I decorate my house, clean it, and cook many meals for others. I can worship as I travel on planes, trains, and automobiles, as I teach God's Word to women. I can worship as I speak and write books. It has been a true joy to see *all* my words as worship, and *all* my work as worship. I rejoice that I now see my pain as a sacrifice to bow before my Lord in worship.

Worship is the lifestyle of a grateful heart. To worship is to respond, to respond to a Lover who always loves and always draws near. What is my love response to the One who has given all? I can only bow before Him every day.

I bow my knees.
I bow my words.
I bow my attitude.
I bow my work.
I bow my times of waiting.
I bow my pain.
I bow my will.
I bow ONLY to HIM.

As I bow before my Lord every day, I have discovered some wonderful benefits.

THE BENEFITS OF WORSHIP

In my early years as a Christian, my passion was for my purpose — to serve, to minister to people, to disciple. Now I have a passion for God Himself! God has changed me from a servant to a worshipper. Does this mean I no longer serve others? No. In fact, I serve *more,* but my service flows from a different place — from a heart saturated with worship, from a heart drenched with the presence of God.

Worship has also deepened and expanded my prayer life. Prayer flows more naturally; it flows out of worship.

Worship has elevated my choice to obey God. Obedience has taken on a higher purpose. In the past, I memorized many convicting passages from Proverbs and James about my words. I wanted to honor God with what came out of my mouth. Of course this pleased the Lord, but, oh, the difference now that I understand that my words can literally be as worship!

As I've learned to walk my worship, I have grown spiritually. I have always longed to know God's voice to me personally, and now His voice is louder and I hear His personal words to me. The joy of God's presence is a daily reality. My heart is fixed on worshipping the Holy One. I see all of my life as worship, and this is transforming who I am.

I was thirsty, and God satisfied my soul with deep intimacy with Him.

ARE YOU THIRSTY?

Are you thirsty? Do you know why? Perhaps like me you are stretched thin with weariness. Perhaps like me you are desperate for God's presence and a vital intimacy with Him. Or maybe you feel just a little bit thirsty, or are not sure what you feel. Wherever you are, I invite you to come with me on this exciting adventure of knowing Christ intimately and basking in His presence.

Come, learn about the specific act of worship and drink from God's well of delight. You will find it oh so satisfying to your soul!

Come, learn about worship as a lifestyle. As you understand how to bow your words, work, pain, and every area of your life, obedience will become a joy.

Worship!

> It's what angels do.
> > It's what Satan wants from us.
> > > It's a major theme in the Bible.
> > > > It is why we were created.
> > > > > It draws us into the presence of God.

I worship God all day, every day. I find such joy and freedom that it is difficult to express in a few words all I am learning about worship. It would take a whole book — and so that is what I have written. You are holding that book in your hands.

So, my friend, will you join me on this journey?

Do you want to have your life changed? *Become a worshipper.*

Do you want to know the presence of God? *Become a worshipper.*

Do you long for deep, soul-satisfying, face-to-face intimacy? *Become a worshipper.*

The call goes forth:

Come, let us worship and bow down,

Let us kneel before the LORD our Maker. (Psalm 95:6)

My
Worship
Awakening

Chapter 2

My Worship Awakening

All the earth will worship You,

And will sing praises to You;

They will sing praises to Your name.

PSALM 66:4

This week my husband and I watched the captivating movie *The Miracle Worker*, which is about the life of Helen Keller. Deaf and blind, Helen existed in a cocoon of unknowing and could not comprehend even the most simple things about life. She was asleep to the joy of communication, learning, and understanding. Helen grew, and with each year she became more isolated and frightened. In desperation, her parents hired a teacher, Anne Sullivan, to try to break through Helen's cocoon and help her interact with the world around her.

One of the most gripping scenes in the movie shows a frustrated Anne Sullivan holding Helen's hand and repeatedly spelling out words with sign language. Helen doesn't get it.

On the verge of giving up, Anne spells out w-a-t-e-r over and over to Helen. She pulls Helen into a brook and spells out w-a-t-e-r as she splashes the crystal, cool liquid over her, but Helen cannot grasp the connection between the name and the wet substance. Anne gives Helen a drink of refreshing spring water. Still no recognition.

Then Helen pumps water from the well — LIGHT — joyous light! The cocoon bursts open. Helen awakens to the truth that w-a-t-e-r *is* water! One minute she knows nothing, the next minute the world is alive to her. She erupts from her cocoon of unknowing into a world of love, relationships, and intellectual understanding.

Like Helen, I was asleep, but not to w-a-t-e-r and knowing the physical world we live in. I was asleep to w-o-r-s-h-i-p and the spiritual world, where God's presence is a living reality. I wanted to wake up to face-to-face intimacy with God. I wanted to wake up, to be alive to His presence. I wanted all He is to be enlarged in my awareness. I wanted to be overwhelmed with God!

In this chapter and the two to follow, I want to show you what awakened me to worship and God's presence. These chapters will discuss the specific act of worship, where I bow my knees and declare, "Holy, holy, holy." I want to show you from my experience and from the Word how God broke through my cocoon and breathed new life into my relationship with God through worship.

First, let me tell you how I grew in awe, astonished wonder, and adoration of God.

GROWING IN AWE

Scripture was key in giving me a deeper understanding of God's holiness. Two passages were significant, and the Lord wrote them in bright neon letters across the landscape of my heart and mind. I knew both of these passages, but He opened my eyes to see them in a new way.

Seeing God High and Lifted Up

The first passage was 1 Chronicles 29:11-14, where David blesses the Lord before the Israelites by lifting Him high and declaring that everything belongs to God. Greatness, power, majesty, and splendor are God's. Everything in heaven and earth is God's possession, and He rules and is exalted over it all. David declares that everything he possesses is a gift from God, and that what he gives back to God was given to him by God in the first place. These glorious truths cause David to worship: "Now therefore, our God, we thank You, and praise Your glorious name" (1 Chronicles 29:13).

As I said, I was well-acquainted with this passage, but as I memorized and meditated on it, God stirred up my heart. No words can describe how my Father spoke this passage to me. It was as if He took His hand and imprinted the words on my spirit. I told Him, *Greatness, honor, power, splendor . . . it's all yours, my Lord. Truly every material thing I possess . . . my home, my food, my new pair of shoes that I love, are from you. My husband, children, grandchildren, and friends are gifts from you. My spiritual gifts, abilities, are given by you. Lord, I can only give back to you what is already yours. Like David, I can give you my worship — I can declare day and night how glorious you are!*

The second passage was Isaiah 6, a passage I'd read hundreds of times. I'd meditated on it, even taught it, but then God took those same words and breathed new life into them for me.

Isaiah was a man who understood much about God. He had become familiar with the good things God had created, but he had never been introduced to the presence of the Holy One. Isaiah 6 clearly portrays what happens to a person who is in the mystery of the Holy Presence.

> In the year of King Uzziah's death I saw the Lord sitting on a throne, lofty and exalted, with the train of His robe filling the temple.
>
> Seraphim stood above Him, each having six wings: with two he covered his face, and with two he covered his feet, and with two he flew.
>
> And one called out to another and said,
>
> "Holy, Holy, Holy, is the LORD of hosts, the whole earth is full of His glory."
>
> And the foundations of the thresholds trembled at the voice of him who called out, while the

temple was filling with smoke.

Then I said,

"Woe is me, for I am ruined! Because I am a man of unclean lips, and I live among a people of unclean lips; for my eyes have seen the King, the LORD of hosts."

Then one of the seraphim flew to me with a burning coal in his hand, which he had taken from the altar with tongs. He touched my mouth with it and said, "Behold, this has touched your lips; and your iniquity is taken away and your sin is forgiven."

Then I heard the voice of the Lord, saying, "Whom shall I send, and who will go for Us?" Then I said, "Here am I. Send me!"

(Isaiah 6:1-8)

Isaiah received a startling, glorious vision of the Lord, high and lifted up. Seraphim called out, "Holy, Holy, Holy," and Isaiah was undone. The foundations trembled, and Isaiah, overwhelmed, convicted, and humbled, could only respond, "Here am I, my Lord, send me!" What glory Isaiah saw! What a privileged view of the Exalted One! Would I like to be given such a vision? Absolutely. And I expect you would too.

Yes, I had read this passage a hundred times or maybe several hundreds of times, but then I read it yet again. In my journal I wrote:

Today something amazing happened as I was meditating on this holy passage. I saw the Lord seated on the throne exalted. I did! Was it a "real vision"? No. I didn't see with my eyes, but with my spirit. And I was overwhelmed with God. I laid my Bible aside and fell prostrate, weeping. As

I listened to Matthew Ward's beautiful song of
Isaiah 6, "I See the Lord," I felt my foundations
trembling, and like the prophet Isaiah when he
saw the King, the Lord of Hosts, I could only
confess and reaffirm, "Lord, here am I, send me."

I think of worship as spirit-to-Spirit communication. In worship my spirit flows to His and His Spirit back to mine. That day as I read Isaiah 6, God spoke to me through His Word. He spoke to me through a beautiful song of worship and He communed with me, spirit-to-Spirit. In the past I had studied about God's holiness, but on that day I encountered the Holy One. Ever since then, I long to bow my knees in worship.

Isaiah saw God high and lifted up, and Isaiah was undone. Looking *upward,* he encountered the holiness of the Almighty, and this trembling prophet fell to his knees. Whenever we see the holiness of God, we are forced to look at our lack of holiness. Looking *inward,* Isaiah was overcome by his own sinfulness. Graciously, God cleansed Isaiah's heart, and then he was able to look *outward* and respond to God's call to "go."

Isaiah was changed.

So was I.

May I ask you a question? Have you ever been brave enough to pray, *God, I want to see you high and lifted up; I want to encounter your holiness?* A. W. Tozer, one of my favorite writers, said that we need to, because "God has been abridged, reduced, modified, edited, changed and amended until He is no longer the God whom Isaiah saw, high and lifted up."[1] May we see Him as He is, the God of eternal excellence. May we stand in awe of Him.

Do you want to be awestruck before God? I encourage you to read Isaiah 6, as if for the first time. Read this passage with new eyes, asking God to give you a vision of Him as high and lifted up.

When you see God as high and lifted up, your response will be to bow before Him.

Bowing Before Him

When we see God's holiness, our response is deep respect and reverence. For me, this means bowing my knees before Him, as David invites us to do in Psalm 95:6.

"Come, let us worship and bow down, let us kneel before the LORD our Maker."

Did you know that the definition of *worship* wonderfully expresses the act the word describes? *Worship* comes from the old Anglo-Saxon word *weorthscipe,* which was modified to *worthship,* and finally to *worship.* I wish it had not been shortened because "worthship" is what worship is about; to worship is "to attribute worth" to something or someone.² So a good definition of *worship* is: an active response to God that declares His worth. These strong action words are synonyms for worship: *adore, admire, celebrate, esteem, exalt, glorify, love, magnify, praise, revere, reverence,* and *venerate.*

The Hebrew word *shachah,* translated in the Old Testament as "worship," means to fall prostrate or bow down. When you worship, you are literally prostrating yourself before God. You are submitting your intellect, your future, and your arrogance to God. Watchman Nee says it like this: "In worship I acknowledge my limitations. In worship I also acknowledge that God has no limitations. I bow before Him. He is beyond me in everything."³ When I bow, I submit my sense of superiority, because to worship is to acknowledge an inferior before a superior.

In various countries, people show respect with the body:

In Korea and Japan — These dear people bow constantly in respect to one another, bobbing up and down like ducks on the lookout for fish. When my husband and I were teaching in Korea, a young man greeted me with a deep bow, I bowed back, and he again bowed. I had no idea how long the bows were to continue. It felt strange, but helped me see the connection between bowing and respect.

In England — When the Queen of England passes by, what do

the people do? They bow out of respect, often all the way to the ground.

In the United States — When the president walks into the Senate Chamber, what do the senators do? They stand to honor the President.

Standing and bowing are ways we show respect, honor, and worship with our bodies. When I stand in worship — bow, kneel, fall prostrate, or lift my hands to praise the Holy One — I am saying by my actions, *God, you are better than I am. You are bigger than I am. You are more than I am. I yield to your ways, they are higher than my ways. I yield to your time schedule, it is better than mine.*

When I worship God (in private or in public), it is difficult for me to "sit and worship." If I sing, "You are glorious," I want to declare God's glory with my body as well as with my words.

I am watching God change my new friend Bev from a *servant* of God into a *worshipper.* I asked her what she has learned about bowing to God in worship. Here is her answer in an email.

Bev:

I imagine myself bowing before the King of kings, who is also my Father, seated on His great throne. Then I picture myself as a child bowing my head on my Sweet Abba's lap while He gently tousles my hair. I worship Him by giving praise for all that He is and thanksgiving for all that He's done, most importantly for adopting me into His family.

I often open my Bible and praise God as I read through one of the psalms. It doesn't come natural for me to submit my will to Him because I like to be in control. So as I ask Him to help me bow my life before Him, I lower my face to the floor and spread out my hands in an act of submission. I

picture myself bowed before His feet, like Mary
when she poured out costly perfume in a generous
act of love. In this posture of humility I am better
able to give up all of me to gain all of Him. He
fills me with His presence, and I am overcome
with delight. In this humble state I am lifted up
and filled with indescribable love for my Faithful
Father, Compassionate Savior, and Loving Holy
Spirit.

Like me, Bev's awe of God causes her to bow before Him in
worship.

I am also growing in astonished wonder. I can't give you a
one-two-three formula of how God began to expand my heart to
the glory of His creation. I simply asked Him to draw me nearer,
and He began to give me a delighted, childlike wonder over His
creative creation.

GROWING IN ASTONISHED WONDER

I can identify with this quote from A. W. Tozer:

There is a point in true worship where the mind
may cease to understand and goes over to a
kind of delightful astonishment — to "transcen-
dent wonder," a degree of wonder without limit
and beyond expression. It is always true that an
encounter with God brings wonderment and
awe.[4]

The godly Bishop in Les Misérables knew this astonished
wonder. Victor Hugo summarizes the Bishop's everyday life as
follows:

The Bishop's day was full to the brim with good
thoughts, good words, and good actions. Still the
day was not complete if cold or wet weather pre-
vented him from spending an hour or two in the
garden before going to bed. . . . He was alone with
himself, collected, peaceful, adoring, comparing
the serenity of his heart with that of the Other,
affected in the darkness by the visible splendor of
the constellations, and the invisible splendor of
God. . . . He dreamed of the grandeur and presence of God. . . . Without seeking to comprehend
the incomprehensible, he gazed at it. He did not
study God: he was dazzled by Him.[5]

King David knew this deep place of worship. Never before
had a man worshipped as David did. Perhaps never since. He worshipped seven times a day, continually, in the midst of trouble and
in and out of tragedy. The Psalms is a biblical hymnal, and David's
heart flows over its pages. When David saw creation, he saw God.
And he worshipped. When lightning raced through the sky, David
did not see just a piercing light. He saw God's arrows. When thun-
der rolled through the sky, David heard God speaking. David read
nature as a parable pointing him to a higher reality, the wonder of
God.

Listen to his words in Psalm 19:

The heavens declare the glory of God;
    the skies proclaim the work of his hands.
Day after day they pour forth speech;
    night after night they display knowledge.
There is no speech or language
    where their voice is not heard.
Their voice goes out into all the earth,
    their words to the ends of the world. (verses 1-4, NIV)

God's creation shouts forth His praise. The language of nature needs no translation — it transcends every language, communicates in every country. David was an astonished man, filled with wonder over all God had made. He saw the trees clapping their hands with joy, the waves lifting their hands in worship, the fields dancing, and the mountains bowing. To David, all creation was a symphony breaking forth in praise to the Mighty One.

I am learning to let God astound me with the wonder of His creation — and, oh, the delights I've encountered. Let me tell you about a few of them.

> ❦ A few years ago I was on a hike to reach the waterfall behind my home. As I climbed over boulders, I saw that a pine tree had been toppled by a recent, violent storm and was obstructing my view of the waterfall. As I hiked around the fallen tree, I thought, *How sad, this tree will die.* But I was wrong. Each time I made the hearty hike to the waterfall, I found the pine tree bowed over, but still thriving and green. It lived because its roots went deep down into life-giving water.
>
> One day when my heart was discouraged and tears my companion, I climbed to the pine tree and quietly sat. Then I prayed, *God, you have allowed the storms of life to topple me on my side like this pine tree, but, my Father, push my roots down deep in your Word, into your life-giving water that I too may thrive and stay green.* God spoke to Moses through a burning bush, and He had spoken to me through that pine tree.
>
> ❦ Every Easter I traipse through the spring snows in search of the first flowers. As their buds brave the inclement weather, push up through the snow, and open their petals to the sun, they shout, "He is risen!

Lift your heart, lift your hands to Him!" When I encounter these brave wildflowers, I tell my God, *Let me be willing to push up through the cold ground of life — let me open "my petals" to you and praise you. Let me see the beginnings of spring, not just the cold of winter; help me move forward rather than retreat.* I'm glad no one can see me singing and talking to flowers! But they bring joy to my heart and turn my eyes in worship of my great God who faithfully serves up spring every year.

❧ When I gaze at the pale lavender and white columbine, Colorado's state flower, I see God's glory. This long-stem, fragile sprig of a flower is sheltered in the rocks, and I find its delicate beauty hidden in cool, refreshing places in the forest. After discovering a field of columbines, I wrote in my journal: "Thank you, my Father, for allowing me the privilege of gazing on these hidden treasures. Draw me into the shelter of THE ROCK, hide me in your presence so that your delicate beauty shines through my life."

❧ Last summer, Jody and I pulled a blow-up mattress onto our deck so we could sleep under the stars. I couldn't sleep because the canopy of stars was shouting the praises of the Holy One.

I so long to grow deeper in astonished wonder. For too long I raced through life with my eyes straight ahead, not pausing long enough to look down at the flowers or up at the twinkle of the stars. When you see the heavens, do you see the glory of God? Do you experience astonished wonder at God's creation? If not, stop racing long enough to turn your gaze up and ask the Father to pour wonder into your heart.

It's a prayer He loves to answer.

When I first began to go before God in private worship, I sometimes wondered why I was worshipping. I would walk in the glory of God's creation, fall on my knees, and praise God: "You are holy. Your creation is magnificent!" I would wait in silence and then think, *Why don't I feel anything?* My spiritual senses were not tuned to God's presence in creation.

We know that the body has senses and that our physical senses can be quickened through use. For instance: Joni Eareckson Tada, a quadriplegic, trained herself to paint by holding a brush in her mouth. In *How to Worship Jesus Christ*, Joseph Carroll tells of a badly burned man whose sight was gone and he was taught to "read" the Bible in Braille with his tongue.[6]

Just as the body has senses, so does the spirit. By the senses of our spirit we are made conscious of the presence of Christ. We cannot see God with our physical eyes, touch Him with our physical hands, or hear Him with our physical ears, but the senses of our spirits can see and touch and hear Him.[7] Just as our physical senses can be quickened by practice, so can our spiritual senses. I know, because my spirit is being trained to perceive the presence and wonder of God. I am growing sensitive to His voice. I see Him with the eyes of my spirit in a breathtaking, new way. I believe that with practice, you can too.

My worship awakening not only involved growing in awe and in astonished wonder. I also grew in adoration.

GROWING IN ADORATION

Did you know that worship originates in God's great love for us? My Abba (which means Daddy) loves me with abandoned delight, and He longs for me to be abandoned in my love for Him. Much of the time when I went to God in the past, saying, "I love you," in the back of my mind I had a long list of what I wanted Him to do for me. I was centering on my need, not on God.

Then the blessed Holy Spirit began to change my thinking and my life. He had to, because the Holy Spirit is profoundly committed to restoring the first commandment to first place in our lives. He longs that we grow in adoration of the Holy One. God wants us to pray and be thankful, but I rarely went beyond thanking God to being consumed with Him. Oh, I longed to go deeper in loving my God for Himself and not for what He could give me.

God spoke to me through A. P. Gibbs's words about worship, which pierced my heart. "In prayer we are occupied with our needs, in thanksgiving we are occupied with our blessings, but in worship we are totally occupied with God Himself."[8] As I read those words, I "heard" God saying, "Wake up, Linda, wake up! I want you to be alive to me. I long for you to know how deep my love is for you. And my desire is that your heart will burst with love for only me."

I had loved God since becoming a Christian at age twenty, but something new began to stir in my heart; it went beyond loving Him. I grew to adore Him. I started to long to be with Him. I began to understand what David meant when he said, "My soul thirsts for you, my body longs for you (Psalm 63:1, NIV). Often the One I loved would wake me in the night, and I would get up and trust my sleep to Him. I yearned to be with Him, to "hang out" with Him, to bask in His presence as my father, friend, and lover.

I am old enough to remember when churches began to move from singing hymns to singing praise choruses. One of the first praise choruses was: "Father I Adore You." I can remember standing in church, singing this chorus, looking at others singing, and thinking: *Does anyone here really adore the Father? Adore* is such a heartfelt expression. Do you *adore* God?

I like what Tozer wrote about adoring God.

The admonition to "love the Lord thy God with all thy heart . . . and with all thy mind" (Matt. 22:17) can mean only one thing. It means to adore Him. I use the word *adore* sparingly, for it is a precious word. I love babies and I love people, but I cannot say I adore them. Adoration I keep for the only One who deserves it. When we adore God, all of the beautiful ingredients of worship are brought to white, incandescent heat with the fire of the Holy Spirit. We love Him with fear and wonder and yearning and awe. When we adore Him, worship becomes a completely personal love exchange between God and the worshipper![9]

I too now reserve the words *adore* and *awesome* solely for God alone. Does the thought of adoring God make you squirm? How about kissing God? Before you think I am really going off the deep end, let me tell you that the Greek word in the New Testament for worship means "to kiss toward."[10] It is almost the idea of blowing a kiss to God. Rarely do we think of adoration and kissing in relation to God. Neither do most of us think of crawling up into the Father's lap, but that is exactly what my favorite quote about worship says.

Ultimate worship takes place when we, like children, find ourselves climbing into the lap of our heavenly Father with the desire just to be with Him. At that moment there is no agenda other than to sit in His presence, to love Him, to whisper in His ear our gratitude, to feel His face, to hear His heart, to rest in His embrace, to enjoy the moment, and to understand more fully the God who yearns to enjoy us.[11]

Worship is our love responding to God's love. When we become aware of that love, our responses are worship responses.[12] And the beautiful thing is God comes to us when we worship!

Psalm 22:3 says that He comes in a very special way. My Bible translates it, "God is enthroned in the praises of His people." Other English translations say, "God inhabits the praises of His people." In the Japanese Bible, it says: "When we worship, we build a big chair for God to sit in." I love that! My worship invites the Holy God to come and dwell in the big recliner my worship creates for Him. I invite His presence. My worship speaks to God's heart, *Holy God, I love you. I worship and adore you. Come, sit in this chair I'm building for you. I'll climb into your lap, put my arms around you, and hug you.*

As I work in my home, I talk to my Lord of my deep love for Him. Our house has two staircases, so I'm constantly walking up and down stairs. Every trip up or down is my signal to turn my heart to worship and pour out words of adoration. Up the stairs: *Oh, Lord, I love you today. I love you with all my heart, soul, mind, and strength.* On the trip down: *Oh, Holy One, my heart bursts with love for you. All day long I speak of my love to my Lover.* My favorite place to be is in my Abba Father's lap, with my head nestled against His heart.

Come, Let's Get Practical

You've read about my worship awakening. Now I'd like to invite you to worship with me. Right now, if it is possible, kneel with this book before you. I want to take you through a worship experience I call the "ABCs of Worship." Will you join me in exalting Him?

Begin worshipping God with a word that begins with A and say, "My God is awesome," and then declare other attributes of the Father that begin with A. Perhaps, "God, you are Abba Father."

My Holy One, you are:

A   Awesome, my All in All. I adore you!
B   Beautiful, Bountiful, Bold, Blessed are your names.
C   My God, you alone are the Creator, the Christ, the Coming One.

D   Deliverer, you are my delight.

E   Eternal One, Excellent, Everlasting One!

F   My Father, Faithful One, Forgiver of my sin.

G   My God, you are great, glorious, the Giver.

H   Holy, Holy, Holy, my God, you alone are holy, high, and exalted.

Continue through the ABCs from I through Z (X and Z are a challenge). Every time I go through the ABCs of worship I am overwhelmed anew at ALL my God is. I pray you too stand amazed before Him. If you have children at home, consider worshipping through the alphabet with them. If they are young, help them think of attributes of God and write them down together. Then worship together with just three or four letters. Or go for a walk with a friend and praise God in this way. Your hearts will be refreshed, renewed, and revived as you give worship to your King.

May our great God awaken our hearts to worship Him! Will you pray? *Holy One, draw me to you. Let me see you high and lifted up in all your glory. Give me astonished wonder over your creative creation. Teach me the great joy and privilege of bowing my knee in worship and declaring, "You, O God, are worthy!"*

Chapter 3

——

My
Soul
Finds
Stillness

Chapter 3

My Soul Finds Stillness

Be still, and know that I am God.

PSALM 46:10, NIV

I often worship God with the ABCs of Worship, and most days, the words come faster than I can speak them:

Almighty, Amazing, Abba

Benevolent, Brilliant, Beautiful

Captivating, Creator, Conqueror

But it hasn't always been that way. About ten years ago, when I was diligently working to make the shift from being a busy, serving Martha to a contemplative, sit-at-His-feet Mary, a simple exercise like the ABCs of Worship could turn into an exercise in frustration.

I remember one such time when I knelt on the floor, intent on quieting my heart and worshipping my heavenly Father through the words that describe who He is. My worship went something like this:

"A. Awesome Lord, I adore you more than words can express. You astound me." *How did that stain on the carpet get there? It wasn't there yesterday. Jody must have walked in here after he'd been working in the yard. Oh well . . .*

"B. Holy One, you are my Beloved, my Bounty Giver . . ." *Barney, quit barking. Maybe someone's at the door. Should I go check? Hmm. No doorbell. Must be a deer or a rabbit. Now where was I . . . ?*

"C. Caring. Comforting. Creative." *It's hot in here. Maybe I should open a window. No, focus, Linda. Focus.*

"D. Divine. Delightful . . ." *Daughter! Oh, God, please direct my*

51

*daughter as she makes a decision about adopting a child. She desperately needs
your direction. God, my mind is drifting today. . . . Oh well, at least I'm using
D words. Then there is Dinner and Dry cleaning. I've GOT to put those on my
to-do list. Oh dear. Lord, why am I so distracted?*

D is for distractions. Easily distracted — that was me.

As I began to grow in awe, astonished wonder, and adoration
of God, excitement filled my soul over all I was learning about
worship. But I had one big problem — I didn't know how to stop
the treadmill of my life so I could get off and discover stillness.

Why did I need a quiet heart? Because we cannot realize true
intimacy with God until we learn to come before Him in quietness of spirit, mind, and body. God's Word paints pictures of this
wonderful state of stillness. David said, "My soul waits in silence
for God only" (Psalm 62:1). Habakkuk declared, "But the LORD is
in His holy temple. Let all the earth be silent before Him" (2:20).
When Elijah waited for the voice of God, the Lord was not in the
consuming earthquake, or the blazing fire, but in "a still, small
voice" (1 Kings 19:12, AMP).

One of my favorite verses in Psalm 46 encourages me that
when I am still, I can enter into an intimate knowing of God:

> Be still, and know that I am God; I will be exalted
> among the nations, I will be exalted in the earth.
> (verse 10, NIV)

The Hebrew word for *know* in this verse is *yada*, which is used
to describe the most intimate kind of knowing between a husband
and wife — the kind of knowing in sexual intercourse. It is the
same word used in Genesis 4:1, "And Adam *knew* Eve as his wife"
(AMP, italics mine).

Do you see what God is saying here? You and I can *know* Him
in such an intimate and personal way that we share a deep spiritual oneness with the Creator of the universe. In this special intimacy, His Spirit indwells us, His breath inspires us, and His heart

invigorates us.[1] When we are still, we can discover face-to-face intimacy.

This is what I longed for. I believe it is what you desire too. So I asked the Lord, *Why can't I be still? Why do I see the carpet stain, dry cleaning, and dinner when I long to focus on You?*

As I searched my heart, I realized that the outward clamor of my busy life and the continual inward chatter caused by restlessness had kept me from the blessing of stillness and the felt presence of God.

BUSYNESS — EXTERNAL CLAMOR

In the days of *Little House on the Prairie*, women battled busyness, but the external clamor of their lives was centered in one place: their home. They had lots of children, constant activity, and I'm sure they were weary much of the time. Theirs was a physical exhaustion from their hard labor.

In this age of constant stimulus, clamor is pervasive and comes from many sources. I am tired, but not from physical labor. My tiredness comes from the frantic pace of life around me. Yours likely does too. As I look at my friends and at myself, I fear we are becoming nervous, anxious, overactive people who don't know how to be still. We rarely give our full attention to anyone or anything. We're always thinking ahead to the next thing that must be done, the next person we must talk to and check off our list. We do the same with God. We hurry to our "Quiet Time," which is anything but quiet. Our bodies sit, but our minds race. Ready to get on with the day, we hope our moments with God win His approval.

When a journalist asked Thomas Merton what he considered to be the leading spiritual disease of our time, Merton's answer surprised his interviewer. Of all the things he might have suggested (lack of prayer, lack of community, poor morals, lack of concern for justice and the poor), he said, "Our problem is not so much badness as it is busyness."[2]

In *Making All Things New*, Henri Nouwen gives a good word picture of today: "Our lives often seem like over-packed suitcases bursting at the seams. In fact, we are almost always aware of being behind schedule. There is a nagging sense that there are unfinished tasks, unfulfilled promises, unrealized proposals. There is always something else that we should have remembered, done, or said."[3]

Nouwen's right. Before my worship awakening, my life was a bulging suitcase. If the suitcase began to look of normal size, I scrunched more into it. Martha (of Mary and Martha fame) also lived a crammed-suitcase-kind-of-life.

THE MARTHA MENTALITY

You probably know the story of two of Jesus' favorite people, Mary and Martha, and how they each chose to love Him (see Luke 10:38-42). I like how Martha Kilpatrick describes these two women: "Jesus stopped at Bethany one day and Martha bustled to fix His lunch and make Him comfortable. She chose to relate to His humanity . . . Martha would feed Him. Mary stilled herself in homage before Him. She chose to relate to His divinity . . . Mary would feed *on* Him."[4]

Picture Martha: scurrying back and forth around the kitchen. Chop, chop, chop. Dice, dice, dice. Pour, stir, fan, bake. Angry. Frustrated. Sigh, sigh, sigh.

Picture Mary: peacefully sitting at Jesus' feet, adoring Him with her soft eyes. Worshipping Him in stillness. Blissful. Peaceful. Sigh.

Martha made one choice; Mary chose something else. Perhaps it had something to do with how God had made them. Mary was one type of personality — a contemplative thinker; Martha was another type — an active doer. My personality matches Martha's, and like Martha, for most of my life I chose duty. But Mary made the better choice. She chose devotion. She chose Jesus.

For thirty years I asked God to change me into a Mary. I longed to want to sit at Jesus' feet. I asked with very little faith, because deep down in my soul I was convinced it was impossible. Why? Because I'm an off-the-charts extrovert. On personality tests (Myers-Briggs, Taylor Johnson), I test as an extreme extrovert. I'm also a doer — doing comes easy for me. I like doing. I am good at doing, and I feel good about myself as a doer. I check many items off my to-do list, and red checks make me feel good. I accomplish a lot. I help people. I am appreciated.

When I first read Martha Kilpatrick's book about Mary and Martha, *Adoration,* I thought, *This is about me. This is my story.* Especially piercing were these words about the treasure of time.

> Time is the treasure of life. Time IS life.
> Time is the willing sacrifice that you offer up to
> The worship of what you love.
> Don't tell me what you love. Tell me where you
> spend your TIME and I'll tell YOU what you
> love.[5]

Before my worship awakening, my life showed that I loved serving others. My time was spent "doing" for Jesus. Now my time is spent "being" at His feet, worshipping Him. I am proof that God can take a Martha and transform her into a Mary. How I praise Him for the joy!

You may be a distracted, busy Martha or a more reserved, contemplative woman who knows how to avoid the pitfalls of hectic busyness. But do you know how to handle the restlessness created by internal chatter? Few women do.

RESTLESSNESS — INTERNAL CHATTER

At one time four children roamed the halls of our home. Distractions were the norm. But even when the kids were in school, a flurry of activity existed — not all from without but from *within me*. This internal chaos has a name — restlessness. Even when I was alone and could be quiet before the Lord, I couldn't turn down the volume of internal chatter. *Linda, in this hour you can call five women, write five emails, prepare the Bible study, start dinner, throw laundry in the washing machine*... How could I center on the Lord when my mind wouldn't stop?

I wanted to be still, but I didn't know how. While *restlessness* is easy to define, *restfulness* is more difficult. Two painters each painted a picture of their concept of restfulness. The first chose to paint a still, lone lake amid some far-off mountains. The second painted a thundering waterfall with a fragile birch tree bending over the foam. At the fork of the branch, almost wet with the pounding water, sat a robin on its nest.[6]

Is there a woman alive whose life is like the first painting? I doubt it. Do you know anyone whose days are filled with the stillness of a placid lake among the mountains? I don't. My life — and the lives of women I know — feel very much like a thundering waterfall. The violent spray of water constantly, continually pounds on us, and we have no "turn off here" button to push.

Restfulness is a form of awareness, a way of being amid the noise of life. It is being in my ordinary, busy life with a sense of ease, gratitude, appreciation, peace, and prayer.[7] It is the robin sitting peacefully on her nest, *perched on a branch above* the thundering waterfall.

I wanted to become like the robin. I longed for stillness in the midst of real life. I had too many jobs, not enough hours in my day, and an aging body (despite my telling it to STOP!). Then God began to teach me about stillness.

A PORTRAIT OF STILLNESS

One of my favorite psalms is Psalm 131. Only three verses long, this psalm of David's paints a picture of stillness.

> My heart is not proud, O LORD,
>> my eyes are not haughty;
>> I do not concern myself with great matters
>> or things too wonderful for me.
> But I have stilled and quieted my soul;
>> like a weaned child with its mother,
>> like a weaned child is my soul within me.
> (verses 1-2, NIV)

The Message makes verse two come alive: "I've kept my feet on the ground, I've cultivated a quiet heart. Like a baby content in its mother's arms, my soul is a baby content."

I love the picture in these verses, but at first it confused me. I didn't understand why David said that a stilled and quiet soul was like a *weaned* child. Why not a *nursing* child? I remembered the nights when my babies woke, longing for my breast. Their little mouths frantically searched until they found the source of comfort and sustenance. In contrast, when they were weaned, they no longer looked to my body as a means of satisfying their hunger, and could be content to simply lie in my arms.

David could be still before God because he no longer came to the Lord with a "gimme" spirit. He longed only to climb up in his Father's lap and calmly nestle against His heart. He had found quietness and happiness in intimate communion with God.

I often pray Psalm 131, and when I do, I think of Rachel, a young woman I met at a conference where I was speaking. Words poured from Rachel's lips. Hard words. Difficult words to hear. *Rape. Pornography. Abuse.* "My mother sold me to men for a joint."

I clasped sobbing Rachel to my breast, wishing with

everything inside me that I could hug out the pain in her
heart. Without realizing what I was doing, as I held her, I
began to rock back and forth. For fifteen minutes, seated
on the stairs leading to the altar of the church, I became
the mother Rachel desperately needed. We rocked. Rachel
sighed. A sigh of quiet peace. A sigh that said, "I am held.
Someone cares. I feel loved."

The next day Rachel found me. I knew what she wanted. I
held out my arms to hug her again. We rocked and she sighed. I
thought of Psalm 131: "But I have calmed and quieted myself, like
a weaned child who no longer cries for its mother's milk. Yes, like
a weaned child is my soul within me" (NLT).

Rachel longed for God to hold her like this. It was my longing
as well, so I prayed: *My Father, teach me to be still like Rachel, to come to you
and let you hold me and rock me until I sigh in quiet rest.*

For me intimacy with God begins when I quiet my heart, stop,
and know that He is God. At rest, I snuggle against His heart. I
sigh. I listen and He speaks to me through His Word and by the
Spirit. In the stillness, I discover intimacy with Him and hear His
voice. And sometimes when I am still, He takes me to a place of
deep worship, a place I call *the silence of the soul.* I describe this place
in my journal.

> Today, while I was in the presence of the Holy
> One, He revealed to me the joy of deeper wor-
> ship. I am not sure I can express in words, they
> are so inadequate. Words minimize the beauty,
> the joy, the intimacy, the holiness, but I must try.
> My prayer is ever, *Lord, take me deeper. Take me deeper
> in what it means to worship you. Take me deeper into your
> presence.* And today He did! I had been reading
> in 2 Chronicles, where twice the presence of the
> Holy One descended with such heavy glory that
> the priests could not work because of it.

Amazingly, on my knees in worship, I experienced a glimmer of this. I was struck with such a stunned silence, an utter quiet before Him. I could not move, I could not speak or raise my hands in worship. I could only bow as low as I could bow, completely overcome with HIM — with His majesty, with His holiness. I just wanted to stay in the silence, under the cloud of His presence. Afterwards, I tried to work, but I could not. I could only walk around and enjoy the afterglow of His presence; only softly repeat, "I love you, I love you, I love you."

When God, in a beautiful way, silenced my soul in His presence, I was not seeking an *experience*, I was seeking *God Himself.* My purpose was to give Him honor and thanksgiving and praise. He chose to manifest Himself to me in a precious and overwhelming way. If God grants us experiences with Himself, we rejoice and thank Him, but our purpose must be to bless Him, to seek *Him*, not what He can give.

Through Psalm 131, and many other passages, God showed me the link between being still and knowing Him . . . *really* knowing Him. In the stillness, I began to hear His voice to me, personally. O. Hallesby described well why stillness is necessary in order to hear God's voice: "The greatest blessing connected with stillness is that we can hear eternity; we can hear the voice of the Eternal One as He speaks to our conscience."[8]

What does it look like for you to be still and know God is God? Please, don't ignore this question. Take time to form an honest answer, because doing so could change your life. It certainly changed mine!

COME, LET'S GET PRACTICAL

What follows are practical ways that you can stop the external clamor and internal chaos in your life so that you can learn to worship God in the stillness. The word *still* can be an acronym for how to experience stillness:

S   Seek stillness
T   Take a retreat
I   Increase prayer
L   Let go of external clamor
L   Learn the Twenty-Minute Worship Experience

1. *S — Seek stillness.* I have never had days when hours of quiet automatically appeared in my life, calling out to me to enjoy the stillness, and I doubt you have either. We have to be intentional about stillness. Even Jesus knew that solitude and stillness would not simply appear, so He was committed to seeking stillness. While He lived in inward "heart stillness," He frequently sought outward stillness. He spent forty days alone before beginning His ministry (see Matthew 4:1-11) and a night alone with His Father before selecting His disciples (see Luke 6:12). Stillness was a regular practice of Jesus'. It is also a regular practice for my friend Mimi, whom I told you about in chapter 1.

Mimi:

> When I was thirty years old and the mother of three little ones, I made a choice to become a worshipper. I realized that my mind would need the greatest corralling, so I found a spot in the house that I could go each time I worshipped. That special place spoke stillness to my soul. I

soon learned that all I could offer God was my desire. It was a revelation to realize I could not even worship without His help. If I worshipped in other places in the house, I soon found places to dust and this distracted me. So I developed a plan. I made Monday my "Day of Worship."

I decided not to accept any appointments for Monday morning. (If something unplanned came up, I found another morning to worship.) I began at 9 a.m., after making sure the children were happy with activities. All week, I would look for things that would best occupy them during my time of worship. Even the finding of things for my children to do became part of my love gift to my God.

I would start the laundry and my bread-baking before I started worshipping. However, I soon found my mind filled with things I needed to do that week, so I kept paper and pen by my side so I could write those things down and then continue to worship. I stopped my worship every hour to see that all was well. I changed the loads of wash and finished my bread-making, and then went back to worshipping.

My goal was to spend two to three hours alone with God to adore Him. At first I did not know enough about Him to worship that long, but I would read His Word, talk to Him about my life, and offer Him the things I owned . . . my sphere of influence. I was offering Him access into my world.

That was twenty-eight years ago. I still have a daily time of worship, but now the house is quiet. Now my worship is an ongoing interaction.

How can you, like Mimi, seek stillness? By looking for "little solitudes" during your day.[9] Consider the quiet moments when you first wake up (unless the baby wakes you up first!). Reflect on the delight of a steaming cup of coffee in the morning. Sit down, breathe deeply, and tell the Lord you love Him.

You can enjoy a "little solitude" in the midst of bumper-to-bumper traffic. You have a choice; you can worship or get irritated. If you have children in the car, put on a kid's worship CD and worship with your children.

Ask the Father to help you recognize the "little solitudes" in your day, such as when you are nursing your baby, folding the laundry, or during your children's naptime. He will open your eyes to opportunities for worship.

2. T — *Take a retreat.* All my life, if I had a free day, I spent it ministering to women. But God has changed this extrovert. As I write these words, this former Martha is at Praise Mountain, alone with her God. This prayer and fasting retreat is a respite for my soul. Alone for three days, I am reveling in the quiet. I have come to worship the One I adore. I can't remember ever having three entire days alone with my God. No phone, no email. No food to prepare, no people to talk to. Just my God and me. Joy, unspeakable joy!

I am at a place in life where I can go away for three days alone. How does a busy young mother or a woman who works forty hours a week find time to take a worship retreat? I've asked two friends to tell you what has worked for them.

Phyllis: A Four-Hour Retreat

> When my four children were young and the noise and activity level in our home was deafening, it seemed impossible for me to find time to be alone with the Lord. I could find time for everyone else, but how could I create time to retreat with the One I loved?

Then the Lord put on my heart that I should schedule an "Escape with God," just as I scheduled time with family and friends. I set aside one day a month for worship. I got a babysitter, created fun things for the kids to do with her while I was gone, and escaped for aloneness with the One I loved.

Often I went to a coffee shop and leisurely drank a cup of coffee while reading my Bible. Then I would go on a walk and talk to my Lord as I walked. For four uninterrupted hours all the clamor of my life and chaos in my mind was stilled. I was revived, refreshed, and renewed in His presence.

Darlene: A Twenty-Seven Hour Retreat

I have a special needs daughter, Amber, who is autistic and mentally challenged. As Amber entered her teen years, she became mentally ill and needed twenty-four hour care. My life was continual clamor and chaos, so I cried out to the Lord, *Please show me where I can find stillness.*

The Lord answered my cry for help. It was as if He said to me, "Come away my beloved, come away and be with me alone." So, once a month I began to go away (to a hotel or to a friend's spare room) from about noon on one day till around three on the next day.

These times became so precious to me . . . a time of realigning myself with True North! I would sleep if I needed to sleep, but I would still have plenty of time to worship and study entire books of

the Bible. I guarded this time so tenaciously that
if I was not fasting, I would often bring my own
food so I didn't have to leave my "holy of holies"
until it was time to return home.

How was Darlene able to leave her responsibilities for twenty-seven hours? Her husband took over all her home duties during that time. She says, "I realize that not all husbands are as gracious as mine, but if we can prove to our husbands how much this time would increase our effectiveness as wives and mothers, perhaps some would reconsider!" (Remember, you don't have to take a retreat once a month — start out with once a year!)

3. I — *Increase prayer.* To delight in the quiet whispers of prayer, we must have stillness. Richard Foster wrote a prayer of quiet that speaks to the outward clamor and inward chatter of our lives. Why don't you pray this prayer every day for a week?

The Prayer of Quiet

I have, O Lord, a noisy heart. And entering out-ward silence doesn't stop the inner clamor. In fact, it seems only to make it worse. When I am full of activity, the internal noise is only a distant rumble; but when I get still, the rumble amplifies itself. And it is not like the majestic sound of a symphony rising to a grand crescendo; rather, it is the deafening din of clashing pots and clanging pans, what a racket! Worst of all, I feel helpless to hush the interior pandemonium.

Dear Lord Jesus, you once spoke peace to the wind and the waves. Speak Your shalom over my heart. I wait silently ... patiently. I receive into the very core of my being Your loving command, "Peace, be still." Amen.[10]

One of the enemies of communion with God is a frantic mind, swirling with other things. It's almost impossible to hear the voice of God when you're constantly hearing your own chatter. What do you do if while praying "The Prayer of Quiet" your mind begins making a grocery list instead of meditating on the Lord?

- Keep a notebook nearby and download on paper any thoughts that distract you.
- If your mind won't quiet down, read a psalm or other passage of Scripture out loud.
- Worship or pray out loud.

4. *L — Let go of external clamor.* When I come to my secret place to meet with God, I try to block out everything that will distract me. I go to my outdoor sanctuary, or to my office, and fall to my knees and ask God to teach me to be still. Often I pull a prayer shawl over my head to keep out light and all distractions. I put on earphones with worship music to shut out noise and pull me into God's presence.

I've asked my friends Bev and Kim to tell you how they let go of external chatter.

Bev:

> I am not an auditory learner and am easily distracted, so any background noise causes me to lose focus. I have found it can be easily muffled with earplugs, so when I go into my special place of worship (my den) and fall on my knees before Abba, I take along a good pair of earplugs. Once the plugs are in place, I can be still and worship.

Kim:

My boys are four, six, and eight, and I work thirty-two hours a week at a hospital that is continually filled with noise as well as emotional trauma. Many days I have returned home from work exhausted, and when I open my door, I hear loud music and see three wild boys running around. Needless to say, there is not much stillness. If I wait for still moments in my home or even at my job, I would be quiet before the Lord maybe once a week, and that time would be interrupted ten times! Stillness is not about the environment around me; it is about the environment within me.

I learned when the boys were very young (and screaming in the back seat of the van as we drove down the highway) to put myself in a "zone." The zone is in my mind, of course. I mentally create a box around my entire person, where nothing gets in but Jesus. When I'm in my zone, I am enveloped in Christ. Sometimes I envision a glass shield between the back and front seats of the car. I can see the boys, so I know they're safe, but their noise does not reach me. When I turn on worship music, it helps me focus my heart on Him in worship amidst the chaos around me.

5. *L — Learn the Twenty-Minute Worship Experience.* As I close this chapter, I want to introduce you to an exciting worship experience that brought me to stillness and the presence of God. I believe this project can change your spiritual experience. I call it the Twenty-Minute Worship Experience. I asked my precious friend Becky to

share with you how this challenge revolutionized her walk with God.

Becky:

When Linda challenged me to spend the first twenty minutes of my time alone with God in praise and worship, I had no idea about how it would impact me.

The first morning, I put on some soft worship music, knelt down, and begged the Holy Spirit to be my teacher. I knew I couldn't do this alone. Even though God felt far away, I began to praise Him for what I knew to be true about His character. As I praised Him for His attributes, a mysterious thing began to happen. His presence came close. It's not that God moved. Rather, it was as if He awakened my soul out of deep slumber to rise up and enjoy His presence. My circumstances didn't change. The trials I faced still loomed (I had breast cancer and a crisis had splintered my extended family), but these problems had shrunk in comparison with God's glory.

The twenty minutes flew by and I found myself longing for more time in worship. And day after day I continued. Sometimes, I allowed worship music to prompt my praise. At other times I went for a walk and allowed the beauty of God's creation to inspire my worship. At times all I could do was kneel and weep in His presence. Pouring out my sorrow at His feet, I bowed before His holiness. When I felt too weak and worship felt too hard, I lay on my face before the Lord, and prayed Scripture back to Him, asking the Holy Spirit to make the truth of His Word come alive in my heart.

As I faithfully worshipped every morning, I began to change. The Holy Spirit began to draw my heart into deeper union with His. I experienced the love of God more intensely. I began to hear His voice more clearly and embraced His purposes more readily. I found myself growing more courageous and less fearful. Through Linda's challenge, I discovered my deepest desire — in the stillness of worship, I found His presence.

Now it's time to challenge you. I challenge you to bow your knees for twenty minutes each day for the next month. This is a suggestion, not a law. Ask God if the Twenty-Minute Worship Experience is right for you or if at this stage of life, yours should be a Ten-Minute Worship Experience.

Here are a few suggestions for your worship time:

- Ask God to teach you about worship — just be still before Him.
- Pray "The Prayer of Quiet," or write your own.
- Pray Psalm 131, asking God to reveal to you how your soul can be stilled.
- Put on a headset and worship with worship music. Sing or say the music to your God.

If you commit to daily worship, I believe that like Becky and me, you will discover stillness and be changed. My prayer is that you will grow in intimacy with God and bask in His presence.

Chapter 4

Expanding
My
Worship
Experience

Expanding My Worship Experience

Come, let us worship and bow down,

*Let us kneel before the L*ORD *our Maker. For He is our God.*

PSALM 95:6-7

Come with me to beautiful, historic Cambridge, England. As you stroll through the manicured university grounds, allow the cobblestone streets and stone-hewn buildings to transport you back to another place and time, a simpler place void of high-tech hurry and information overload. Notice the Thames River as it meanders through the city and along the outskirts of King's College. Take in the breathtaking view of the stately stone cathedral. Enter through the twenty-foot ornately carved doors and walk into the sanctuary with its high ceilings and walls of wood so dark they seem almost black. The caliginous wood and soft candlelight create an ethereal ambience, enveloping you in the whispers of yesteryear. A holy hush hovers in the air.

My husband, Jody, and I are here, in the sanctuary of King's College, to attend Evensong, a time of prayer that is sung. Every weekday in the late afternoon, the heavenly voices of The King's Choir sing the Psalms or The Magnificat (Mary's psalm of praise). In the candlelight and alongside Jody, I bow my knees on a kneeling bench and fold my hands in prayer. Nearby sits an altar adorned with a majestic painting of the Christ child by Rubens. The pews are set against the sides and I kneel, facing other people, not the altar. A whispered reverence fills the room and I thank

God for the joy of joining other worshippers in this place. I worship in holy awe.

Now, come with me to another place where I experience the specific act of worship — the contemporary World Prayer Center in Colorado Springs, Colorado, a circular building made of steel and glass with a blue roof. Flags representing different nations surround the building. On Wednesdays I join worshippers from forty different churches for an hour of worship in this modern, floor-to-ceiling glass edifice that looks out at Pikes Peak and the Rocky Mountains. A communion table adorned with bread and grape juice sits off to the right and people serve themselves at their leisure. One man stands at a keyboard at the front of the room, calling out to worshippers, inviting us to worship the living God through song and celebration. Some worshippers shout praises and lift their hands. Others kneel in the aisle, contemplating His majesty. All feel free to praise God through a multitude of expressions. I join these exuberant men and women as they praise the King of kings. I worship in joyful celebration.

Ready for another place where I worship? Come with me to a splendid cathedral crafted not by human hands, but by the Master Builder, a sanctuary made of mountains, pine trees, sky, rocks, wind, sun, and water. In this expansive setting behind my home at the foot of the Rocky Mountains, I take a "holy hike." With my water bottle, faithful dog, and iPod filled with worship music, I climb up to the trail that winds around Raspberry Mountain, then hike again to a waterfall. I am alone in God's cathedral, walking and worshipping, walking and talking with my beloved Father. Often I find a place to bow my knees in the forest, but even as I walk, I bow my knees in an attitude of heart. I thank God for the joy of joining Him alone in His creation. I worship in holy splendor.

Now come with me to a special room in my home, my upstairs office where there is a kneeling chair that a dear friend found for me in Ecuador. In this room I study God's Word and write, answer emails, and talk on the phone. But at times, this room ceases in its office role and becomes instead my private sanctuary as I turn off the telephone and computer, put on my worship music, and bow my knees before my God. Whether in the middle of the night, or the middle of the afternoon, this time alone with my Father is the most important time of my day. I bask in His presence. I adore Him. And I listen for His voice. *Lord, speak. Your bondservant listens.* Often, the time on my knees follows my time in the Word, and I praise the Holy One with the Scripture I've been studying or memorizing. How I thank God for the joy of being with Him in my private sanctuary. I worship in holy peace.

The last worship experience I want to tell you about is not focused on a place but rather on a person, the friend I told you about in chapter 1, Lorraine Pintus. Lorraine and I worship together often. Sometimes we take holy hikes. Other times we are on our knees by the couch in my office. Often we are in a hotel room as we travel for a speaking engagement. Wherever we are, we kneel before God as we listen to two or three praise songs on my CD player. After worshipping our Beloved with song, we worship Him with our words. We whisper words of adoration for who He is and offer thanksgiving for what He has accomplished. Prayer flows naturally from our worship. (We have spent much time praying for you — for every woman who will read *Satisfy My Thirsty Soul.*) How I thank God for the privilege of going to His throne with a friend, where together we see the Holy One high and lifted up. I worship in holy fellowship.

Prior to my worship awakening, I believed that the act of worship only took place on Sunday mornings in church. I now understand that we can worship God anywhere, and that we can worship in community or in solitude. I've had many sweet times with the Lord, in different places and with different people, times when I've experienced such a welling of His life and presence that I was overwhelmed. Environment certainly influenced these moments, but my sensitivity to God's voice and presence is far more important than the actual place.

Several things expanded my understanding and practice of worship, particularly these truths that Jesus taught about the act of worship and that David taught about worshipping with the body:

- ꙮ Prayer flows out of worship.
- ꙮ Because God is Spirit, He must be worshipped in spirit and in truth.
- ꙮ The body is to be an instrument of praise.

Let me explain what I learned about each of these that has affected how I worship.

DISCOVERING THAT WORSHIP AND PRAYER FLOW TOGETHER

When the disciples asked Jesus to teach them about prayer, He gave them the Lord's Prayer. He said, Pray like this:

> "Our Father which art in heaven,
> Hallowed be thy name.
> Thy kingdom come, thy will be done
> in earth, as it is in heaven.
> Give us this day our daily bread.
> And forgive us our debts,
> as we forgive our debtors.
> And lead us not into temptation,
> but deliver us from evil:
> For thine is the kingdom, and the power,
> and the glory, for ever. Amen."
> (Matthew 6:9-13, KJV)

We often repeat this beautiful prayer in our worship services, but it is also a pattern for prayer. Jesus' words, "Pray like this," (NLT) mean, "Pray according to this pattern." What is the pattern? Start and end prayer with worship. The essence of prayer is worship! You may be surprised to discover that of the sixty-eight words in the Lord's Prayer, thirty-six are words of worship. More words of worship than of request, this is the Lord's pattern of prayer.

Look carefully at this famous prayer of Jesus', and you will see that the first three statements concern God's honor, while the second three concern our interests. Andrew Murray points out that our pattern of prayer often reverses this order:

> There is something here that strikes us at once. While we ordinarily first bring our own needs to God in prayer, and then think of what belongs to God and His interests, the Master reverses the order. First, *Thy name, Thy kingdom, Thy will*; then, give *us*, lead *us*, deliver *us*. The lesson is of more importance than we think. In true worship the Father must be first, must be all.[1]

Throughout most of my Christian walk, prayer was a weak link in my chain of devotion to God. I prayed, but no one would have called me a prayer warrior. But when God began to change me from a servant into a worshipper, I became a woman of prayer, because prayer began to flow naturally out of my worship. Jesus' pattern became my pattern.

Sometimes I pray the Lord's Prayer, but most often I personalize it and pray "according to the pattern" — something like this:

> *My Father — oh, it is so wonderful that you are MY Father. I love how that sounds. Your name is holy, so holy. May your kingdom come here on the earth, Father, and, oh, I long for your will to be done — in the world — but also in my little world. I want to bow my will to yours today. Gracious One, I ask that you give me what I need today, lead me away from anything that*

would tempt me to forget you. Guard and deliver me from the
Evil One. Oh, my Lord, yours is the kingdom, all the power, and
the glory for ever and ever. My Father, let it be so.

I encourage you to bow your knees before your Father, asking Him to teach you how worship and prayer can flow together in your life.

Now, let's move on to the next principle that expanded my worship experience — learning to worship in *spirit* and in *truth*.

LEARNING TO WORSHIP IN SPIRIT AND TRUTH

One of the most penetrating discussions about worship occurred at Jacob's well between Jesus and the much-married Samaritan woman. (See John 4:1-42. It would be good for you to read this passage.) This woman was looking for the proper way to worship, but she saw only two options — the Samaritan method or the Jewish method. The Samaritan method was enthusiastic heresy; they had *spirit* but not *truth*. The Jewish method of worship was barren, lifeless orthodoxy — they had *truth* but not *spirit*.[2] In this encounter Jesus sets up a different model for worship by informing this woman that both ways of worship were unacceptable. He tells her:

> "But an hour is coming, and now is, when the
> true worshipers will worship the Father in spirit
> and truth; for such people the Father seeks to
> be His worshipers. God is spirit, and those who
> worship Him must worship in spirit and truth."
> (John 4:23-24)

Several important ideas emerge from this passage. First, Jesus says that we are to worship the *Father*. This astounded the woman, because the Old Testament, which was the Scripture of her day, doesn't refer to God as Father. To view God on such a familiar level was foreign to her thinking. Next, Jesus reveals that the Father *seeks worshippers*. This, too, amazed the Samaritan woman — God needs nothing, but He still seeks worshippers? Third, Jesus says that because God is Spirit, we *must* worship Him in spirit and truth. Jesus didn't say, "I would strongly suggest that you worship in spirit and truth, but it's really up to you and how you feel about it." He commanded us to worship in *spirit* and in *truth*.[3] These two elements are an integral part of worship. Let's explore the meaning of this often mentioned but rarely explained concept.

Worshipping in Truth

To worship in *truth* means that I worship truly. It is the opposite of worshipping a made-up god. It is giving the true God the honor of an enlightened mind, one filled with the truth of who He is. To worship in truth, I must know God's Word and be sincere.

1. I must know God's Word.

I worship the Holy One on the basis of my understanding of the truths about Him. Who He is determines how I worship. My knowledge of God limits my worship. If I don't know that He is wonderful, how can I say, "You are the Wonderful One, my Lord"? If I don't know that God's Word states that He is in control of all things, how can I praise Him with, "You are the Sovereign God, the One in whom I trust"? So, to worship in truth I must first and most importantly fill my mind and heart with Scripture.

The power of memorized Scripture was vividly illustrated to me several years ago. I can still see the tiny one-room house where Jody and I sat on old wooden chairs and drank tea with a pastor and his wife in China. I asked this dear man how he had survived his twenty-one-year imprisonment during the Cultural Revolution without a copy of the Word of God to encourage and feed his soul. I will never forget his response. "Oh, I had much of the Word of God stored in my mind and heart. You see, I had memorized Ephesians, Colossians, Philippians, Psalms . . ." and he went on to name many more books of the Bible. I felt like hanging my head in shame.

2. I must worship with a sincere heart.

A woman who worships in truth comes to the Lord with sincerity, integrity, and purity of heart. To be sincere means to be a woman "without a mask." In ancient times, wax masks were worn to the great masquerade balls given by the kings. To be sincere came to mean "without wax." When business transactions were made, common questions were, "Are you sincere?" "Are you hiding something behind a mask of wax?"[4]

God looks deep within our minds and hearts (see Psalm 7:9). I can imagine Him coming to each of us and asking, "When you sing songs of worship, when you bow or kneel or raise your hands to honor me, are you sincere? Is your worship genuine and authentic? Or are you hiding something behind a mask of wax?"

Worshipping in Spirit

To worship in *spirit* is to worship spiritually. It is the opposite of worshipping only from external rites or rituals. It is giving God the honor of an affectionate heart; this is the passionate side of worship.

1. Spirit worship flows out of my human spirit.

When Jesus says that we must worship the Father in *spirit*, the Greek word indicates He is referring to the human spirit, the inner person.[5] Every person has a human spirit. It is the essence of who a person is; it's his or her very life. Perhaps you have sat by a loved one who has just died, or been to an open casket funeral. If you are near the body, it is obvious that the person — their human spirit

— is not there. Instead there is only a body, a shell that housed the spirit.

Jesus is saying that our human spirit — the intangible, untouchable but real part of who we are — must reach out and touch the Father, who is Spirit, in worship. We are to commune with Him, Spirit to spirit. "The one who joins himself to the Lord is one spirit with Him" (1 Corinthians 6:17). According to Watchmen Nee, "Since God is Spirit, we must use spirit to worship Him."[6]

To worship in spirit means to worship spiritually. We must be spiritual in thought, word, and deed. For me, this means I continually ask God to examine my heart as I pray from Psalm 19:12-14 or Psalm 139:23-24: "Search me, O God, and know my heart; try me and know my anxious thoughts; and see if there be any hurtful way in me, and lead me in the everlasting way."

2. Spirit worship must involve the Holy Spirit.

While every person has a human spirit, not everyone possesses the Holy Spirit. This is an important distinction, because apart from the Holy Spirit, it is impossible to worship God in the fullness of spirit and truth that Jesus described in John 4:4-26 to the woman at the well.

Let me paraphrase their encounter, highlighting their seemingly superficial comments about water, as well as the deeper undercurrents that flow beneath the surface of their words.

She says, "I thirst."

He hears, "I yearn for face-to-face intimacy."

She says, "I've had four husbands, but they have not satisfied my thirst."

He says, "I can give you special water, living water that will become *in you* a perpetual spring from which you can drink so that you will never thirst again. This is spiritual water ... it is from God — it *is* God."

She says, "As a Samaritan, I worship God in this way."

He responds, "I can show you a new way to worship, a way that will satisfy your thirsty soul."

Although cloaked in the beauty of a word picture, Jesus is saying that when the Samaritan woman drinks of Him, the Holy Spirit will be *inside* her. This is why worship comes from the inside out. When the living water of the Holy Spirit infuses our human spirit in worship, it becomes a spring that bubbles up, producing a river of praise that delights the heart of God and blesses us in the process. The same living water that Jesus offered to the woman at the well is available to you and me!

I asked my creative friend Kathy how she saw the intermingling of our spirit with the Holy Spirit in worship. Her answer made me laugh, as she said, "I see it like a candy cane." When I said, "Tell me more," Kathy sent me the following email:

> For some reason the vision of a candy cane keeps coming to me. I have my spirit — the human spirit God so graciously gifted me with — and during worship my spirit mingles with His Spirit. . . . My spirit intertwines with His. And although we are both distinct entities (the red and white), we become one solid force (the candy cane) that cannot be separated. A candy cane would not be a candy cane without both the red and the white spirals, and I would not be a fully human child of God without both my spirit and His. Worship acts as the divine twister.

God is Spirit, so we *must* worship Him in spirit and in truth. God is seeking worshippers who will be ready to follow the adventurous whispers of the Holy Spirit.

Learning to Worship with My Body

Ten years ago I began reading through the Psalms every month. As I read and reread these songs, the picture of worship revealed through David and the psalmists differed from what I had experienced. David hungered for God's presence. While in hiding in the wilderness, he ached to join the throngs in worship. Worshipping *Yahweh* was his lifeblood. Often David's praise was loud, exuberant, and physical. He expressed his worship by bowing, clapping, and lifting his hands in praise. He would kneel, fall prostrate, shout, and dance. This was not my picture of worship.

I believe some Christians are afraid of their emotions, and I was one of them. I could trust God with my mind, but not with my emotions. But as I read and prayed the book of Psalms, God gave me permission to worship with my body. I can't point you to a specific verse that says, "If you worship in freedom, you will experience more joy and delight," but that is what happened to me. As I became free to express my worship with my body, I was filled with more joy.

Am I suggesting that you should change the way you worship? No. I am only sharing my experience and suggesting you read the Psalms and ask God to reveal to you what is right for you. God's Word gives us great freedom in our worship, and His Word, not tradition, is our guide. Nowhere have I seen this more beautifully portrayed than in the following email entitled, "I Saw Joni Dance."[7]

> I was privileged to hear Joni Eareckson Tada speak Saturday night at the Desiring God Conference. Most of you know Joni, a quadriplegic, was paralyzed 38 years ago in a diving accident. She gave a great and convicting message but as the time of worship began, I saw something that was more

impressive than anything I heard. I saw Joni dance.

Joni handles her wheelchair as deftly as any Nascar driver on a racetrack. No sooner had the music begun than Joni began to "dance." As much as a quadriplegic can dance, she danced. Joni has just enough movement and strength in her hands and shoulders to grip the controls on her chair and maneuver herself without the aid of others. Suddenly the chair began to move with the music. She thrust forward, then backward, then forward, then backward. Smoothly, and yet with obvious passion, she turned to the right, then the left, then the right again.

Suddenly, the forward and backward and side to side movements gave way to spinning. Well, as much as a paralyzed person can spin. Joni began to turn her chair in circles, first clockwise, then back again. If she ceased her movements, it was only so that she could lift her contorted hands as high as her paralysis would allow. It wasn't very high, but who's measuring!

I had to ask myself why I often stand like a vertical cadaver. I have the glorious gift and privilege of being able to celebrate God and honor Him with my body. I can kneel, lift my hands to heaven, fall prostrate, clap, and yes, move to the right and left and dance.

I went home thinking about Joni and thinking about her God. What kind of God is this who can inspire such freedom and joy in one who, from a human point of view, would appear to have every reason to hate Him? What kind of God is this who has the qualities and characteristics and attributes and beauty and glory that He can be found worthy of the praise and gratitude and "dancing" of a woman who's spent the last 38 years in a wheelchair? Wow! Now that's some God!

Now that we've looked more closely at the three truths that influenced *how* I worship, let me offer some down-to-earth ways that can help you grow in the kind of worship Jesus described.

Come, Let's Get Practical

1. *Ask God to give you a picture of who He is.* Some Christians I have talked with question using your imagination in worship or prayer. Hannah Hurnard, author of *Hinds' Feet on High Places*, disagrees:

> I believe that the noblest and most glorious and most blessed function of the imagination is to make it possible for the invisible and eternal things to become real to us. . . . Whenever I have a "Quiet Time" and whenever I pray, I imagine the Lord Jesus himself close beside me, and then I speak to him as if I saw him face to face. That makes it easy to talk to him as naturally and simply as I would if I really could see him.[8]

Like Hannah Hurnard, I thank God for the gift of imagination. Often as I bow before Him, I envision the Lord on His Throne, high and lifted up.

I have several friends who also use their imaginations in worship. Becky visualizes God's throne room when she bows her knees in the act of worship. She sees herself kneeling at the foot of the steps that lead to His throne, where He is seated. Martha sees

Christ as King and as the Lion of Judah. Mimi sees herself in a garden, bowed before the Lord, grasping His feet. Phyllis pictures herself as a lamb in the arms of her Shepherd.

2. *Search out special places to worship.* Jesus taught, "When you pray, go into your inner room, close your door and pray to your Father who is in secret, and your Father who sees what is done in secret will reward you" (Matthew 6:6). The same principle applies to worship. Whatever place becomes your "inner room," there you meet the Lord every day to fellowship in solitude with your Lord.

Some places say to my heart, "This is a place of worship." When I climb up to my prayer chair, hidden in the rocks behind my home, my heart is prepared to worship and pray. Why? Because every time I sit in my prayer chair, I pray and worship. The same is true with my holy hike. This trail has *worship* written on it because I always worship there. The couch in my office speaks worship to me because I kneel there in the middle of the night. This couch could tell tales of agonizing tears during worship as well as tears of joy unspeakable. My couch is a place of refuge where I meet my God.

One young mother told me her special place was her walk-in closet. She hides there on her knees with her Walkman pouring praise music into her ears. Another woman said she runs to her large pantry and closets herself with the boxes of cereal to escape the loud vibrations of a young family. Even a walk-in closet or a pantry can become a sanctuary.

Do you have a special place that speaks worship to you? Ask God and start searching, because I'm convinced that He has a place for you.

3. *Find music that lifts your spirit, and allow it to lead you in worship.* The Psalms call worshippers to sing praises to God. "Praise the LORD. Praise the LORD, O my soul. I will praise the LORD all my life; I will sing praise to my God as long as I live" (146:1-2, NIV). Psalm

150 calls for everything that has breath to praise the Lord. The picture is of loud, vibrant music — the sound of the trumpet and the clash of cymbals.

Music is the greatest tool I have found for shutting off the tapes of the day and lifting me above the mundane to the heavens. David packed his harp; the first thing I pack in my suitcase when I leave for a trip is my iPod and little speakers. I transform every motel room into a sanctuary of worship. I turn on my worship music, fall to my knees, and quiet my heart. I worship the Lord with the words of the songs. I go wherever the Holy Spirit takes me. Worship and prayer flow from my worship. Music lifts my spirit to His throne and fills my heart with the joy of His presence.

God has blessed us with modern-day psalmists who lift us to His presence. The same kind of music does not appeal to all. Look until you find Christian artists who speak to your soul.

Worship is all about our amazingly wonderful God. I pray you are encouraged and motivated to expand your worship experience. May you grow as one who bows her knees in the specific act of worship and declares, "Holy, holy, holy!"

In the next chapter, you will begin to learn about the lifestyle of worship, where you bow your life and live holy, holy, holy.

Part 2

Walking in Worship

Chapter 5

I Bow
My
Life

❧

Chapter 5

I Bow My Life

Come let us worship and bow down,

Let us bow our lives in worship before God.

PSALM 95:6, AUTHOR'S PARAPHRASE

Can you see the apostle Paul? I can. He is tired. His hand aches.
He has been writing all night about the glorious mercies of God.
As he reads back over his words that will one day be the first
eleven chapters of Romans, his heart bursts with love for his God.
Laying his quill on the table, he falls on his face before his Lord
and breathes one small word, "Oh!" Just, "Oh!" This little word
declares so much. When we truly see the Holy One, there are no
words, for no words in any language can declare His majesty. Just,
"Oh."

> *Oh,* the depth of the riches both of the wisdom
> and knowledge of God! How unsearchable are
> His judgments and unfathomable His ways!
>
> For who has known the mind of the Lord, or
> who became His counselor?
>
> Or who has first given to Him that it might
> be paid back to him again?
>
> For from Him and through Him and to Him
> are all things. To Him be the glory forever. Amen.
> (Romans 11:33-36, italics mine)

Open your Bible and look. Have you ever noticed the *Oh?* Paul basks in the *Oh* of all God is. His rich wisdom. His breathtaking knowledge. His total otherness. This God-who-became-man is indescribable and unfathomable. All Paul can do is bow. Bow low because everything originates with God, all is given by Him. He is all of life and all of life is Him.

I see Paul slowly stand, throw his hands to the heavens, and declare, "To God be the glory forever. Amen." He sings, in his own words, "How great thou art!" Paul takes his quill once more and ponders. "Jesus, the Christ, gave everything. What can I give in return? I have nothing worthy to give. If I give all my possessions, it will not be enough. If I give my talents, my service, and all my time, it will not be enough. What can I possibly give?"

Then Paul's eyes are opened and he sees: "Ah . . . my life, that's it, I can give my life. I can bow everything before Him as an act of worship. Yes, that's it!" As he begins once again to write, he pens one of the most often quoted verses of the New Testament:

> Therefore I urge you, brethren, by the mercies of God, to present your bodies a living and holy sacrifice, acceptable to God, which is your spiritual service of worship. (Romans 12:1)

I like the way *The Message* makes the verse live: "God helping you: Take your everyday, ordinary life — your sleeping, eating, going-to-work, and walking-around life — and place it before God as an offering." It is as if Paul shouts, "I have something to give! I can surrender my life!"

DISCOVERING THE JOY OF SURRENDER

Surrendering your life to God is very personal, so I am going to ask you to do something important right now. I want you to

envision a big stop sign in front of you. It is a signal to STOP,
LOOK, LISTEN, and THINK deeply about your life. Why
don't most of us think about our life — I mean really think about
it? As one woman aptly put it, "I have too much to do today in my
life to think about my life." But we must. As we read in Psalm 39,
life is brief.

> LORD, remind me how brief my time on earth
>   will be.
>   Remind me that my days are numbered —
>   how fleeting my life is.
> You have made my life no longer than the width
>   of my hand.
>   My entire lifetime is just a moment to you;
>   at best, each of us is but a breath.
>   (verses 4-5, NLT)

Stop and think. When was the last time you thought deeply
about your life? Was it B.C. (Before children) or B.J. (Before job)?
The German philosopher Goethe said, "Things which matter
most must never be at the mercy of things which matter least."
What matters most to you?

Throughout these pages I have asked you questions, but now I
want to ask you the Continental Divide of questions:

IS YOUR LIFE 100 PERCENT SURRENDERED TO GOD?

Be honest when you answer. I'm not asking, "Is Jesus your Savior?"
That is a different question altogether. You can be a Christian,
assured of eternal life with Him, and still not be fully surrendered
to God. This was true for Lorraine (who has great hair and a
pathetic sense of humor). I'll let her explain in her own words.

Lorraine:

I'd been a Christian for fifteen years, and while I often enjoyed sweet, deep fellowship with God, I could not deny that on many occasions a restless undercurrent pervaded my life. I didn't understand this. Jesus promised to give me a peace that surpassed all understanding, so why didn't I have peace?

God revealed the answer through two separate events. The first happened one morning as I was reading the Word. In John 14:9, Jesus and Philip are having a discussion in which Philip makes a rather foolish comment (this I could relate to). Jesus responds by asking, "Don't you know me, Philip, even after I have been among you such a long time?" This verse pierced me as Jesus seemed to ask the same thing of me, "Don't you know me, Lorraine, even after so many years of walking with me?" The question hung in the air — I didn't know what to do with it. I knew a lot *about* Jesus, but did I really, really *know* Him? Something was missing in our relationship.

Several weeks later, I was reading a book in which the author asked, "Are you 100% committed to the Lord?" Obviously, someone who spent as much time as I did at church and in the Word was 100% committed to the Lord. I tried to bypass the question, but the Holy Spirit would not let me read further. The question reverberated in my spirit, "Are you 100% committed to the Lord?" I laid the book aside and forced myself to answer it as honestly as I could. "Yes, Jesus, you are my

Lord. . . . almost. You are Lord of my 98%." I was
98% committed to Him, but there was a tiny part
of myself that I had withheld, a part that was my
out in case God asked me to do something too
difficult, such as endure cancer, or sell everything
I had and move to an AIDS-infested area and
preach the gospel. If He asked these things of me,
I could say "no" because it was in my Two Percent
Box. In that box I had stuffed my worst fears and
doubts, as well as all the questions that God had
not answered satisfactorily, questions like, "If you
are a God of love, why did you take my father from
me when I was seven? If you are so powerful, why
didn't you stop my cousin from committing sui-
cide? And why, after we praised you so joyfully for
the miracle of my friend getting pregnant, did you
allow the baby to be born dead?"

I was horrified to discover how much fear
and anger I'd stuffed into this tiny part of my life.
I argued, "God, I serve you. I pray to you. I do my
best to love and follow you. Isn't that enough? Do
I have to give you everything — even my fears and
doubts and unanswered questions?" Immediately,
the thought came: *I gave everything for you.*

I could not argue that. Yes, He had given
everything for me. He had given His very life.
Could I do less? I bowed my head and prayed.
*God, I'm sick of holding onto this 2 percent. It's making me
miserable. I give it over to you, Lord. My life is yours, nothing
held back. Do with me as you wish.*

Relief washed over me. All my anxiousness
was in my Two Percent Box . . . and that box was
now gone. Oh, the sweet peace that comes with
complete surrender to God, the joy of releasing

my wrestlings to Him. To this day, I've never regretted surrendering my life completely to Him.

Lorraine discovered the joy of surrendering all to the Lord. So did Dr. Walter Wilson.

A missionary once asked this beloved physician and pastor, "Who is the Holy Spirit to you?" He replied, "He is one of the Persons of the Godhead . . . a teacher, a guide, the third Person of the Trinity."

The persistent missionary again inquired, "Who is He to *you?*"

"Truthfully, He is nothing to me. I have no contact with Him, no personal relationship, and could get along quite well without Him." As the words came out of his mouth, Dr. Wilson was deeply grieved.

His friend's reply filled Dr. Wilson with fear. "It is because of this that your life is so fruitless even though your efforts are so great. If you will seek personally to know the Holy Spirit, He will transform your life."

As Dr. Wilson was seeking to understand just what it meant to know the Holy Spirit personally, he heard an Episcopal priest give a message about Romans 12:1 — how each person is to offer their body as a sacrifice and this offering is an act of worship. The priest asked:

> Have you noticed that this verse does not tell us to whom we should give our bodies? It is not the Lord Jesus who asks for it. He has His own body. It is not the Father who asks for it. He remains upon His throne. Another has come to earth without a body. God could have made a body for Him as He did for Jesus, but He did not do so. God gives you the privilege and the indescribable

honor of presenting your bodies to the Holy
Spirit, to be His dwelling place on earth.[1]

Dr. Wilson went home and lay on the carpet in his study,
prostrate in God's presence. Hear his prayer of surrender to the
Holy Spirit.

> My Lord, I have mistreated You all of my
> Christian life. I have treated You like a servant.
> When I wanted You, I called for You; when I
> was about to engage in some work, I beckoned
> You to come and help me perform my task. I
> have sought to use You only as a willing servant.
> I shall do so no more.
> I give You this body of mine; from my head
> to my feet, I give it to You. I give You my hands,
> my limbs, my eyes and lips, my brain; all that I
> am within and without, I hand over to You for
> You to live in it the life that You please. You may
> send this body to Africa or lay it on a bed with
> cancer. You may blind the eyes or send me with
> Your message to Tibet. You may take this body
> to the Eskimos or send it to a hospital with pneu-
> monia. It is Your body from this moment on.
> Help Yourself to it.
> Thank You, my Lord. I believe You have
> accepted it, for in Romans 12:1 You said,
> "acceptable unto God." Thank You again, my
> Lord, for taking me. We now belong to each
> other.[2]

Dr. Walter Wilson discovered the joy of surrender. F. B. Meyer
did as well.

F. B. Meyer was a man greatly used by the Lord. His books are some of my favorites. He heard C. T. Studd, the most famous sportsman in England, give his testimony of why he was turning his back on the world of sports to go to China as a missionary with the China Inland Mission. Studd's famous statement, "If Jesus Christ be God and died for me, then no sacrifice can be too great for me to make for Him," pierced Meyer's heart.

F. B. Meyer went to C. T. Studd and said, "It's obvious that you have something I lack, something that I need. What is it?"

"Have you ever surrendered everything to Jesus Christ?" C. T. Studd asked.

F. B. Meyer thought a moment and said, "Yes, I have." But a small voice within said, "No, you have not."

This conversation deeply troubled F. B. Meyer. Once home, he fell to his knees and began to pray. While praying it seemed as if the Lord came to him and said, "Meyer, I want all the keys to your heart."

All the keys?

"Yes, Meyer, I want all the keys."

Then F. B. Meyer took a ring of keys and handed them over to the Lord. But you cannot fool the Lord. One key was missing. It seemed to Meyer that the Lord began to count the keys and said to him, "There is one key missing; and if I am not Lord of all, I am not Lord at all." The Lord turned to leave the room.

Lord, don't leave! Why are you leaving?

"If I am not Lord of all, I am not Lord at all."

But Lord, it's just a very small key, a very small place in my heart.

"If I am not Lord of all, I am not Lord at all."

In desperation, F. B. Meyer surrendered the last key. This was the crisis in his life. He had to build an altar, and place F. B. Meyer upon the altar. Every key had to be surrendered.[3]

COME, LET'S GET PRACTICAL

You have read how Lorraine gave up her 2 percent, how Dr. Wilson yielded to the Holy Spirit, and how F. B. Meyer surrendered all the keys to his life. What about you? Now is the time God wants you to think about your life. Have you given Him all the keys? It doesn't matter how old you are or how long you have been a Christian. Lorraine was thirty-two when she surrendered her 2 percent. Other women have surrendered their lives when they were in their forties, fifties, or even my age.

As you prayerfully consider whether you are 100 percent surrendered to God, read this thought-provoking prayer of surrender.[4]

> Lord Jesus, I offer you
>> All that I am
>> All that I have
>> All that I do
>> All that I suffer
>> I surrender to you
>> Now and forevermore.

Now, write the following four phrases on a piece of paper in four columns. These can help you think deeply about all you are, all you have, all you do, and all you suffer. Whatever is listed on this page is your personal material for sacrifice.

All that I am   All that I have   All that I do   All that I suffer

Next, find some time this week to be alone with the Lord to think and pray. After you have made your lists, say something like this to God: *Lord, speak to me, guide me. I need to understand what my "life" really looks like, so I know what you are asking me to surrender on your altar.*

Remember, your Father God loves you deeply. He longs for you to hand over yourself—your temptations, temperament, frame and feelings, and all your inward and outward experiences—into His care and keeping, and to leave everything there. He made you and loves you with an everlasting love. He understands you and waits for you to trust Him and to surrender 100 percent of yourself to Him. You could say the prayer Dr. Wilson prayed or Lorraine's prayer of surrender. You could pray the beautiful song, "Take My Life and Let It Be." Or you could pray something like this to Him:

> *Here I am, Lord. I surrender myself to you. I have tried to manage myself and to make myself what I know I should be but have failed miserably. Now I give it up to you. All that I am. All that I have. All that I do. All that I suffer. Take complete control of me. Mold me and make me into the woman you desire me to be.*

Take My Life and Let It Be

Take my life, and let it be consecrated, Lord, to thee;
Take my moments and my days, let them flow in ceaseless praise.
Take my hands and let them move at the impulse of Thy love.
Take my feet, and let them be swift and beautiful for Thee.
Take my voice, and let me sing always only, for my King.
Take my lips, and let them be filled with messages from Thee.
Take my silver and my gold; not a mite would I withhold.
Take my intellect, and use every power as Thou shalt choose.
Take my will, and make it Thine; it shall be no longer mine.
Take my heart, it is Thine own; it shall be Thy royal throne.
Take my love, my Lord. I pour at Thy Feet its treasure store;
Take myself, and I will be ever, only, all for Thee.

— Frances R. Havergal

Once you have presented your life 100 percent to the Lord, the excitement begins. Along with Lorraine, Dr. Wilson, and F. B. Meyer, you have joined in the great adventure of becoming all God created you to be. What you become is your gift to God. Isn't this a marvelous truth?

This truth excited the apostle Paul. He was delighted to realize that he had something he could give God after all — his life. When Paul made the choice to surrender his life as a sacrifice to God, he was bowing his entire life as an act of worship. He then walked out his worship every day by obeying God, which is how we demonstrate our love to our Father.

Our Obedience Demonstrates Our Love

Many passages of Scripture develop the theme of love leading to obedience, including Jesus' words during the Last Supper. Listen to statements from that discourse:

- "He who has My commandments and keeps them is the one who loves Me."
- "If anyone loves Me, he will keep My word."
- "He who does not love Me does not keep My words."
- "If you keep My commandments, you will abide in My love; just as I have kept My Father's commandments and abide in His love." (John 14:21,23,24; 15:10)

These words paint a beautiful picture of obedience flowing from a love relationship with God. Such obedience is a wonderful thing because it is so relational. In Jesus' teaching, *obedience* is a relational term. Obedience flows out of a personal relationship and is motivated only by love.[5] It is a response of love to God. I desire to obey God because I love Him.

As I walk my worship, I am learning of a deep, inner

obedience that comes from nestling close to the heart of my Father. I worship Him and climb up into His lap and cuddle against His chest and hear His heartbeat. I want to cling to Him. I want to bow my life in surrender to Him. I am lifted above rules, above performance, above a have-to mentality. I long to please the One I love.

I am filled with joy because my obedience leads to an experiential knowledge of God and His presence. We all know how the presence of someone we deeply love lifts our spirits and surrounds us with a radiant sense of peace and well-being. So the one who loves God supremely is lifted into rapture as a result of being conscious of God's presence. As A. W. Tozer points out, "Conscious fellowship with Christ is by faith, love and obedience."[6]

Of course, the Lord delights when I tell Him that I love Him, but Jesus made it clear that if my words of love are authentic, I will live out my love by obeying His commands. Obedience motivated by love differs greatly from obedience motivated by duty. Sadly, when many women hear the word *obey*, they think *duty*. The Greek word translated as "obey" is *hupakoe*. It is an interesting compound word of two Greek words, *hupo*, which means "under," and *akouo*, which means "to hear."[7] So if I want to show love to Jesus by obeying Him, I need to practically live out what it means "to hear under."

It helps me understand how to live out my loving obedience if I envision a large, flat rock securely suspended above me. The underside of the rock is filled with light, so when I look up, a ceiling of light hovers above. Atop the rock sits God, who calls down to me. He bends down and whispers words of affirmation, direction, and instruction. I "hear under"—under His love, His protection, and His authority. I may live and move freely under the rock, enjoying all that God has for me there, or I may choose to walk to the edge of the rock, leave the light, and step out into the shadow of darkness. I can live and move in the darkness, but when I do, I am no longer under God; I am under the prince of darkness, Satan. There is no gray area — I am either in the light, hearing under and obeying God, or in the darkness of disobedience. If I want to live out my love in "hear under" obedience, I must stay in the realm beneath the rock, enveloped by the light, under the One who calls to me.

In a state of submission:

I listen for what God is asking of me.

I say "yes."

I obey.

Obedience involves listening attentively with a heart of submission and then obeying God's Word and His voice. The one who hears will comprehend and respond with obedience. But in our wild world of too much to do, how do we stay in a "hearing under" posture? By surrendering every area of our life as a living sacrifice, by walking our worship through obedience.

The Benefits of 100 Percent Surrender

As we bow our life and show our love by obeying, God fulfills some glorious promises.

He Is Intimate with the Upright

God reveals His secrets to those who fear Him.

> The secret [of the sweet, satisfying companionship] of the Lord have they who fear (revere and worship) Him, and He will show them His covenant and reveal to them its [deep, inner] meaning. (Psalm 25:14, AMP)

It has been such a joy for me to watch the Lord reveal His secrets to me. Most often He reveals a "love message" for one of

His women. I was counseling a woman named Tracy, who was in a tragic situation. As I prayed over her, I said at least twice, "God calls you brave and courageous. He is so pleased with the choice you are making." The second time I called Tracy brave and courageous, she stopped me mid-prayer and said, "Linda, did you know the meaning of my name, Tracy?" I had no idea what she was referring to, so I said, "No." She began to weep and told me that Tracy means "brave and courageous," and that she had been specifically praying that she would live her name in the midst of the horrible trial she was going through. How I praised the Holy One for speaking through me and for pouring hope into His wounded daughter.

On another occasion, I walked up to a woman whom I had counseled and said, "Tara, you are in a sexual relationship with a woman." Shocked, Tara said, "How did you know?" I told her I didn't know, but God knew. This so jolted Tara — and proved to her that God loved her and was pursuing her — that she committed that day to become "Tara walking on God's path." I could not stop thanking my God for revealing His secrets to me in order that precious Tara could begin to heal.

What a privilege to have the God of the universe reveal His secrets to you! What joy to be called "intimate friend" of God's! And there is more.

He Reveals Himself

"He who has My commandments and keeps them is the one who loves Me; and he who loves Me will be loved by My Father, and I will love him and will disclose Myself to him" (John 14:21). The word *disclose* means "to manifest, to reveal." *The Amplified Bible* says, "I will let Myself be clearly seen by him and make Myself real to him."

I have come to know the truth of this verse. I have told you that as I grew as a worshipper, I was surprised to find that God's

I BOW MY LIFE   105

presence was hidden in worship. As I have grown in obedience, I've experienced God's presence, and He has revealed Himself to me. His presence has become my delight. (In chapter 12, I will talk more about this, and tell you some of the specific ways God has revealed Himself to me.)

Do you want to know God's presence? Do you long for Him to reveal Himself to you? Then live out your love for Him by obeying His commandments, *and* He will reveal Himself to you.

Our Life Becomes Elevated

Surrendering our life on the altar as a living sacrifice leads us from holy expectancy (the act of worship) to holy obedience (the lifestyle of worship). If worship is *true worship*, it will lead to holy obedience.

The Lord Jesus gave everything for me. What can I do in response except to *offer my life* to Him in return? To surrender every area before my great God and King? I bow my life in worship and my life declares, "Holy, holy, holy!"

As I walk my worship, every word I speak is an act of worship, every task I perform is an act of worship. Each time I bow to God's timeline, I worship. Each time I worship through my pain, I honor my Father. As I do these things, I begin to look at my life differently. My life takes on a higher purpose because I see each action as an opportunity to bring glory to God. My life becomes a beautiful thing because my every action is an act of worship.

In the following chapter you will begin to discover how to bow the individual parts that make up your life. As I wrote these chapters, I gave them to my friend Sandi to read. In an email she wrote:

> Reading the chapters of your new book has been
> so transforming for me. Being able to worship
> Jesus, to bow, with all of my life — work, agenda,

words, pain—is a way I can express my absolute adoration of Him. I have never seen life that way before, and it is so what I long for. It brings delight into everything, from my word choices to my seemingly dead-end job. I'm still not sure of my place in this world (and I'm fifty!), but since I was six, I have just wanted to love Jesus . . . and I can do that with all my life. Yeah!

Turn the page and get ready to learn how to bow your words as an act of worship.

Chapter 6

———

I
Bow
My
Words

Chapter 6

I Bow My Words

Come let us worship and bow down,

Let us bow our words in worship before our God.

PSALM 95:6, AUTHOR'S PARAPHRASE

Have you ever strolled through an old cemetery, paused, and read the words etched in stone as a memorial to a loved one? If you walked up a windswept hill in a country churchyard cemetery in England, you would discover a drab, gray slate tombstone. The quaint stone bears an epitaph not easily seen unless you stoop down and look closely. The faint etchings read:

> Beneath this stone, a lump of clay, lies Arabella
> Young
> Who, on the twenty-fourth of May began to hold
> her tongue.[1]

Can you imagine leaving this "loving tribute" to a mother? Wife? Friend? Most of us wouldn't want a recognition of any variety when it comes to our words. Controlling what comes out of our mouths is one of our most difficult tasks. It took Pambo forty-nine years.

Pambo, who was simple and uneducated, came to Socrates, the philosopher, for instruction. Socrates gave Pambo the thirty-ninth psalm to read. After reading verse 1, "I will take heed to my ways, that I sin not with my tongue" (KJV), Pambo shut the book and left, saying that he would learn that point first.

Several months passed and Pambo was still working on this one verse about watching his words. Socrates demanded that Pambo move forward to another verse. He said that he had not yet learned his first lesson; he gave this same answer when asked the same question — forty-nine years later.[2] Pambo may have been uneducated, but he did not lack for wisdom or perception.

HOW GOD SEES OUR WORDS

If I spend an hour looking up all the verses in the Bible on my words, depression sets in. Like Pambo, I am convinced it will take a lifetime to even begin to make God's truth a reality in my everyday life.

When I open God's Word, I find many convicting passages about my words. For instance:

> My words can stab others, just as if they were stabbed by a sword. (Proverbs 12:18, AUTHOR'S PARAPHRASE)

> My words can bring death. (Proverbs 18:21, AUTHOR'S PARAPHRASE)

Now, obviously, these verses aren't to be taken literally, or there would be a lot of wounded or dead husbands and children lying around. These verses refer to the emotional or spiritual harm our words can cause: the death of the respect of your children when they hear your disrespectful words "stab" the heart of their father, the death of the joy of a child when Mommy stabs him with a sarcastic, critical word. You get the picture — and it's not pretty. But there is another portrait painted in these same verses.

Reckless words pierce like a sword, but the tongue of the wise brings *healing*. (Proverbs 12:18, NIV, italics added)

Death and life are in the power of the tongue. (Proverbs 18:21)

What a contrast: wounds vs. healing; death vs. life. Hope wafts from the last half of these verses. Our words can be filled with life-giving wisdom and the healing balm of encouragement and blessing. When we bless God and others with our words, they are a sweet fragrance of worship to the Father.

Dana longed to be a wife and mother whose words brought life and healing, but instead she felt like a gigantic failure. She often beat herself up over many of the things she said. She tried to do better. She made resolutions, but to no avail. Angry, sarcastic, unkind words toward her husband continued to gush from her mouth. He had deeply wounded her by rejecting her sexually, and Dana used her words as a weapon to hurt him back. But then God began to change her. I'll let Dana tell you:

> I knew my words were wrong, but I couldn't stop them. They had a life of their own. I had studied the convicting Scriptures, read books about the impact of my words, but I was still the same. Then something changed deep inside me. Now, before I go to sleep each night, I think back over my day and picture my words as bowing before the Lord. In the past few weeks, I've observed that some of my words are stubborn — they just don't want to bow down. I've realized that these are the "preaching words" I hurl at my husband that cause him to bristle. . . . I think sometimes

"I'm right" in what I say, but if my words are to
be an act of worship to God, I have to bring those
"preaching words" to their knees (even when I
think I'm right).

What brought about the change in Dana's words? How did
she begin to see her words as a "way of worshipping God"? It
began one day as she and I were talking in my living room. When
she asked me, "What are you studying these days, Linda?" I began
to tell her what God was teaching me about my words from James
and Ephesians. As I talked, God pierced Dana's heart with His
truths. As she saw her words as He sees them, she was motivated
to bow them as an act of worship.

Are you ready to learn more about what Scripture has to say
about our words? I can't promise that you won't be convicted.
These passages have pushed me to my face before God. Are you
still willing? Here goes.

Your Words Can Bless God

God created the world to bring glory to Him. All the earth is to
shout joyfully to God. The waves lift their hands, the mountains
bow down, and the trees clap their hands. Together the instru-
ments of God's design sing the glory of His name and make His
praise glorious (see Psalm 66).

I spoke recently in Alaska, and my room looked out at the
majesty of Mt. McKinley. Over 20,000 feet high, it towers above
the small fourteeners that surround it. One morning I got up
early and went outside to walk and worship (a very cold time of
worship!). I could only think of how glorious it will be to witness
"The All-Creation Symphony of Praise" and to see Mt. McKinley
bowing to the Holy One.

All creation worships, but only God's special creation, man
and woman, can worship with words. You and I have been given a

great privilege, the gift of language. As we do with so many of God's gifts, we often fail to realize the beauty of the gift until it is gone. While playing football in college, my brother, Tom, was injured and unable to speak for six months. Try not talking for six months. Like my brother, you'll become obsessed with communicating with your vocal cords. Yet many of us who can shout, whisper, laugh, and love with our words often become careless with this glorious gift.

Your Words Can Curse Others

The book of James describes the tongue as out-of-control.

> For every species of beasts and birds, of reptiles and creatures of the sea, is tamed and has been tamed by the human race. But no one can tame the tongue; it is a restless evil and full of deadly poison. (3:7-8)

In the Garden of Eden, lions, tigers, grizzly bears, and tongues were tame. But when sin entered the world, the tongue became a wild creature, alongside other beasts. Today trained handlers subdue wild animals, but the wild creature called tongue, no one can tame. But the most tragic part is that we, who have been given the gift of language so that we might worship God, use this gift to curse Him and those who are made in His image.

> With it we bless our Lord and Father, and with it we curse men, who have been made in the likeness of God; from the same mouth come both blessing and cursing. My brethren, these things ought not to be this way. (James 3:9-10)

With the gift of words, we bless God and then turn around and curse husbands, children, and others created in God's image.

This is serious — because when we curse others, we are in effect cursing God and obliterating the previous act of blessing.[3]

Does this make you feel sick to your stomach, as it does me? I've read these verses and thought, *I don't curse people.* But my study of this passage shows that I do. When James used the word *curse*, it meant much more than cursing and swearing. Unkind words about a neighbor, child, husband, or anyone who is made in the image of God count as curses.[4] Ouch!

Are you gulping? I am. How many times after singing praises to God in a worship service have I climbed into the car and spoken unkind words to Jody or our children? How many times have I gotten up from my knees after a glorious time of private worship and snapped at my family?

I find I have something in common with the snail. Did you know that this interesting creature has teeth on its tongue? One small snail, examined under a microscope, had 30,000 teeth on its tongue. The snail keeps its toothy little tool rolled up like a ribbon until it is needed; then it thrusts out this sharp appendage and is able to saw through the toughest leaves with comparative ease.[5]

Our creative God gave snails tongues with teeth because these creatures, who crawl on their bellies, need them for protection and survival. Sadly, some of us who have been given the privilege of speech so that we can glorify God have added teeth to our words. This should not be so.

I warned you God's Word was convicting! But please, don't put the book down (or throw it across the room). I have a few more hard sayings to share from Scripture, and then I promise to give you hope and help.

Your Words Can Be Dirty, Rotten Garbage

First, look with me at Ephesians 4:29-30:

> Let no unwholesome word proceed from your
> mouth, but only such a word as is good for

edification according to the need of the moment, so that it will give grace to those who hear. Do not grieve the Holy Spirit of God, by whom you were sealed for the day of redemption.

Can you imagine the difference in our homes if we could apply just these two verses? We must dissect each one to make sure we understand the important message.

The New Living Translation renders verse 29 as: "Don't use foul or abusive language. Let everything you say be good and helpful, so that your words will be an encouragement to those who hear them." *The Message* says, "Watch the way you talk. Let nothing foul or dirty come out of your mouth. Say only what helps, each word a gift." The use of words such as *foul* and *dirty* are appropriate, as the Greek word (*sapros*) literally means "dirty, rotten garbage." Like bad fruit, "rotten" talk spreads rottenness. If you have ever smelled spoiled fish or garbage left standing in the sun for weeks, the odorous picture is clear. No wonder God commands us to keep foul speech far from us. But what kind of words classify as "dirty, rotten garbage"? Is it only the foul, four-letter variety? Our answer is found in the second half of the verse. The opposite of garbage words are those that edify and bring encouragement. "To edify" means to improve the building's form, to reinforce the structure, so we can say that words that edify reinforce the heart of the person receiving the blessing. Edifying words give grace, not judgment. They meet the need of the moment.

When I lecture (a husband, child, or coworker) instead of love that person with my words, when I push my opinion (which is right, of course!) on a friend, God calls my words "foul." Gossip, sarcasm, unkind remarks, angry words, slander, harsh words — all are foul. The day I realized that my words can cause emotional death was a sobering one. My words can cut open one made in the image of God. But that's not the worst of it.

Verse 30 says that my words can produce an even more ghastly outcome. "Don't grieve God. Don't break his heart" (MSG). "And do not bring sorrow to God's Holy Spirit" (NLT). How do we grieve the Holy Spirit? By our words. Can you picture the Spirit of God grieving because of the dirty, rotten garbage that came out of your mouth today? I can, and I cringe. I don't want to grieve any friend, but I especially don't want to hurt the Comforter and Counselor who dwells in me and leads me into all truth, who reveals the Father to me. Desperate measures are called for and duct tape may not be strong enough. Maybe I should just take a needle and thread and sew my mouth shut.

THE SIN PATTERN IN MY WORDS

My weaknesses are clear to me. Being past the wise age of sixty, I know my tendency to be impulsive, to think that my way is the best way (God calls this pride). I am beginning to see that just as we each have patterns of sinful behavior, we also have a pattern of sin in our words. For some the pattern is sarcasm, for others criticism, for still others negativism. For me it is speaking when I shouldn't. I know the verses, "Those who control their tongue will have a long life; opening your mouth can ruin everything," and "A truly wise person uses few words" (Proverbs 13:3; 17:27, NLT). But still my mouth opens up, and words spill out.

On August 7, 2000, I wrote the following in my journal:

> I was on my knees before my Father — worship-
> ping with the song, "Holy Is the Lord," and I was
> singing with the music, "He is high and exalted in
> majesty." I began to pray, *Oh, my God, let my unspoken
> words exalt you.*
>
>   My request surprised me. Often I pray that
> my spoken words will exalt my God, but this was
> a first to ask that words I chose NOT to speak

would glorify Him. But as I meditated on this, I knew that just as choosing wise words bring Him glory, remaining silent when the words are boiling over to be spoken can also glorify.

When I put a watch over the door of my lips and don't give advice to my husband or adult children (advice that I see as right and just the needed thing), I am worshipping my Father.

When I weigh my words on the scale of wisdom and remain silent, God is well-pleased. It is far easier to talk than to walk my worship. When the words are bursting to come forth, and I wait for God's timing, my words bow in worship before my God.

Very often when I inquire of God, "Should I say this?" His message to me is, "I will fight for you while you keep silent" (Exodus 14:14). Perhaps I am the only one who receives this message repeatedly, because of my sin pattern of saying too much. The problem is, I find it emotionally satisfying to let the words come forth. I feel better; I have had my say. Perhaps this is the issue: Because I want emotional relief, I plunge in and speak quickly — and I get in God's way.

Ultimately, the reason I speak too quickly is things are at a standstill. I know God is working, but He can be so slow, and when His timing doesn't correlate with mine, I'm tempted to jump in and "help Him out." So daily I must bow my spoken and unspoken words before my Lord and say, "My Father, tell me not only what to speak, but when to speak. I long to exalt you with my words."

When we learn to exalt God with our words, they will bring life and healing to others.

THE POWER OF ENCOURAGING WORDS

Well-known author and speaker Larry Crabb tells the following story about when he was an insecure young man with a stutter. In his church, people were encouraged to express verbal prayers to the Lord. Larry wanted to do this, but the thought of praying out loud struck terror in his heart. One day he joined a group of men, opened his mouth, and prayed a prayer that made absolutely no sense. And he stuttered. Humiliated, he plotted to escape before anyone saw him. Just as he reached the door of the church, a hand fell on his shoulder. He thought, *Oh, no, here comes the ridicule.* Turning around, he saw an older man, an elder in the church, and he was smiling. "Larry Crabb, I just want you to know that whatever God has you do with your life, I am 100 percent behind you."

Larry Crabb says that even today, many years later, this story brings tears to his eyes. Someone believed in him! Someone cared enough to speak words of hope and encouragement into his shattered soul.[6]

We are commanded to be encouragers and to build up one another (see 1 Thessalonians 5:11; Hebrews 10:24-25). The word *encourage* in the Greek is the word *parakaleo.* Jesus said that when He went away, He would send us another "comforter," the Holy Spirit. The word *comforter (paraclete)* comes from two Greek words: *para,* which means "with" or "alongside of," and *kletes,* which means a "call." When you put them together, it means that Jesus gave us the Holy Spirit to be in us, to walk with us through this pain-filled life as our Encourager![7] God says that you and I can be a *paraclete,* an encourager to those we love. We can walk alongside a husband, a child, a mother, or a friend and spur that person on, even when life is tough.

Verbal encouragement includes the idea of one person joining another on a journey and speaking words that inspire the traveler to keep pressing on, despite obstacles and fatigue. During the years when the Dillow household had four teenagers, several friends and I decided to do a Bible study on our words in order to better encourage our teens. (I needed all the help I could get with a thirteen-, fourteen-, fifteen-, and seventeen-year-old.) One week our assignment was to say one positive thing each day to our husband and children. That didn't sound too hard. But it was. At our next meeting, one woman said, "Those words sounded so strange in my ears. I realized it was because I rarely said them." Another discovered, "My mouth automatically speaks negative words, gives instructions, and just talks without thinking."

One night when I couldn't sleep, I looked up the English word *encourage*. The root word is *courage*. The prefix *en* means "to put into," so when I tell my husband how much I respect him for responding with love to someone who has hurt him, I put courage into him. What a great thought! I also looked up the prefix *dis*. It means "to separate from." So when I speak discouraging words to my husband, I separate him from the courage he needs to be a godly man. Not such a great thought.

If encouragement does not easily flow from your lips, it might feel as if you're speaking a foreign language when you begin to use words to build up others. But persevere, because words of encouragement give fresh energy to your children and also to your friends.

I was visiting with Kate one day when she opened a file and out poured my letters and cards to her. I was dumbfounded. When Kate's precious daughter became pregnant as a high school senior, I had coveted before God to write my friend at least once a week, but never did I imagine she would save those letters. When I asked her why she cluttered her files with them, she said, "Linda, these letters of encouragement were what kept me afloat. They pointed me to God. I wanted to trust Him, but it was so hard."

Words of encouragement can be spoken or written in letters, emails, or in a hastily scribbled note. One husband's scribble changed his wife's day. I'll let her tell you how his words encouraged her:

Another diaper change for my newborn Zach.
Hadn't there been about a thousand today? It
seemed that way; I was so exhausted and blue. But
as I laid the baby down for changing, I noticed
a note on the stack of diapers. "Zach appreci-
ates it, and so do I." Only one person could have
composed that note — my husband. I noticed
other notes as I walked through the house. On
the washing machine: "Thanks for taking a load
off our minds and off our dirty bodies." On the
stove: "Thanks for great meals."

Encouragement can motivate wives, husbands, children, and
friends to keep on keeping on, even when life is tough. Our children gave my husband a framed letter for his forty-eighth birth-
day. More than a decade later, the letter still sits on his desk. The
title reads, "48 Reasons Dad Is Great!" I remember the day the
kids composed this masterpiece on the computer. From behind
closed doors, laughter continually erupted, and I knew this would
be a special gift. Many of the forty-eight reasons were humorous:
"Dad is great because of his cool hairstyle." (Dad has no hairstyle
as he doesn't have enough hair!) But many were serious: "Dad is
great because he wants his children to live for Christ." I remember
how these written words of encouragement gave this Dad hope
when one of the writers struggled with following Christ. My husband has passed many more birthdays, but this framed letter still
graces his desk.

Now it's time for you to think about applying blessing and
encouragement to the people you love.

COME, LET'S GET PRACTICAL

1. *Have an honest talk with God about your words.* Read James 3:7-10 and
Ephesians 4:29-30 out loud before the Lord, and tell Him how

these verses make you feel. Ask your Father to encourage you and teach you how to bless and encourage with your words.

2. *Memorize a verse this week.* Choose from James 3:9-10 or Ephesians 4:29-30. Ask God to burn His truths into your heart.

3. *Each day this week, covet before God to say one word of encouragement to your husband and children* (if you are single, say it to your roommate, co-worker, or friend). If possible, commit to do this exercise with a friend so you can be accountable to one another.

4. *Consider how you would rewrite Proverbs 12:18 and 18:21 so a child could understand them.*

> There is one who speaks rashly like the thrusts of a sword, but the tongue of the wise brings healing. (Proverbs 12:18)

> Death and life are in the power of the tongue, and those who love it will eat its fruit. (18:21)

Share your simple paraphrase of these two verses with your children. Have a discussion with them around the dinner table about how your family can practice bringing life and healing to others with your words.

5. *Read Ephesians 4:29-30 and ask God to reveal the sin pattern in the words you speak.* Is it sarcasm, criticism, negativism, or lying? Is it speaking too many words? Spend some time praying to God about your area of sin and ask Him for the strength, power, and motivation to change.

6. *Check your tongue temperature.* Ask yourself the three questions that Amy Carmichael, godly missionary to India, asked before she spoke. These three simple, yet profound questions helped her glorify God with her words:[8]

Is it kind?

Is it true?

Is it necessary?

Can you imagine the difference it would make if we lifted each word to God and asked these questions? Our homes would be havens of peaceful interaction, our families would be blessed, and we would be at peace with ourselves.

WILL YOU BOW YOUR WORDS?

When I was studying the power of words, I was amazed at the intimate link, both negative and positive, between the Holy Spirit and the words we say. "Do not grieve and sadden the Holy Spirit by your rotten garbage talk" (Ephesians 4:29-30, AUTHOR'S PARAPHRASE), and "Be filled with the Spirit, speaking to one another in psalms and hymns and spiritual songs, singing and making melody with your heart to the Lord" (Ephesians 5:18-19). When we choose to allow the Holy Spirit to fill us, we will encourage others with life-giving words. We will delight the Spirit of the Living God, who indwells us. Does this thought thrill your heart as it does mine? My words can literally delight God!

But remember, bowing our words as an act of worship is not easy. It is a sacrifice. An offering.

Years ago, a young mom was making her way across the hills of South Wales, carrying her tiny baby in her arms, when she was unexpectedly overtaken by a blinding blizzard. Swirling sheets of snow blanketed the hills. Black fog turned day into night, and she knew she could not reach her destination. Slowly, deliberately, she removed each piece of her outer clothing and bundled her baby boy snugly, first in her hat, gloves, and scarf, then in her sweater and heavy coat.

Exhausted by the wind and cold, the young woman eventually fell, unable to get up and continue walking. Still she managed to hold her child to her chest, protecting him from the cold with her body. When the blizzard subsided, searchers found her buried beneath a mound of snow, but as the rescuers lifted her frozen body, they heard a faint cry. As they unwrapped layer upon layer of protective covering, to their great surprise and joy, they found a baby boy, alive and well! This mother had given her life for the son she loved.

Years later that child, David Lloyd George, became prime minister of Great Britain and one of England's greatest statesman.[9]

Many of you moms would do the same thing for your child. You would take off your outer clothing and use it to lovingly wrap your child in protection from the cold. You would give your life for your most precious possession.

Will you seek this week to give life with your words? God has given you the glorious gift of words, and every day you have a choice to use them to bring:

- Blessing or cursing.
- Encouragement or discouragement.

When you bow your knees to your Father and say, "You are holy, You are worthy, You are faithful," you bless God. It is an act of worship. When your words pour encouragement into your husband, children, grandchildren, friends, or coworkers, you bless others. This too is worship to your great God. Bowing your words is a lifelong journey. Will you begin today to pray?

Oh God, I am desperate for you. Holy One, I long to give life, healing, and encouragement with my words. I have so far to go.

Empower me Holy Spirit. I need you, oh, I need you to pour encouragement into me so I can pour it out to others. May my words become worship to you, my God.

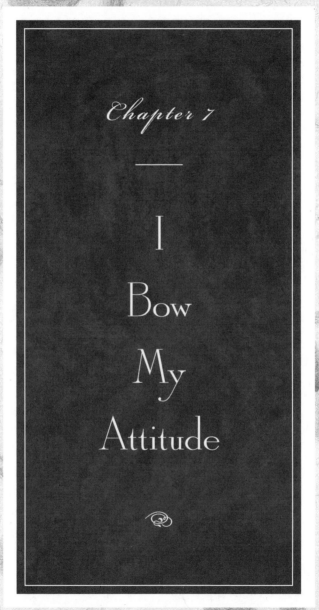

Chapter 7

—

I

Bow

My

Attitude

I Bow My Attitude

Come let us worship and bow down,

Let us bow our attitude in worship before God.

PSALM 95:6, AUTHOR'S PARAPHRASE

I was excited about the day — not a day to stay home and be in my office or kitchen, but a day to be with friends, to go out to lunch and Wednesday Worship together. And then it happened. The huge Christmas tree in our great room perilously toppled and crashed to the floor. My happy spirit plummeted along with the tree. I had asked Jody to check the tipping tree before he left for the office, but the single-focused man had not transferred his attention from computer to tree. Now my priceless, one-of-a-kind ornament from Hong Kong lay shattered on the floor.

I was mad. Mad at the computer that had hypnotized my husband, mad that he was gone and I had to somehow get the massive tree up and balanced between the sofa and wall. Mad that I had to sweep up broken ornaments. Mad at my husband who couldn't get out of his left-brain focus and relate to real life, where Christmas trees and wives fall over.

I swept and prayed, vacuumed and prayed, drove the freeway and prayed, but my spirit still wasn't right. As I approached the exit for the World Prayer Center, I saw it was closed. My irritated spirit erupted out of my mouth. "Closed! I can't believe it. I'm going to be late." Now I was angry at a freeway exit! At that moment the Spirit convicted me, and I prayed, *Oh, God, forgive me. My grumbling attitude isn't pleasing to you. I've been blaming everyone and everything, but the issue is my heart. I long to worship you with my attitude.*

Hanging in my laundry room is a plaque that says *Thou Shalt Not Whine*. I should have placed the plaque in my car and repeated it over and over so I wouldn't whine on my way to worship. Many of us who live in the United States feel we have "the inalienable right to whine." We are commanded to give thanks in everything, but too many Christian women choose to live with a grumbling attitude. We fail to consider the choice we are making.

Let's define the word *attitude*. "Attitude is our mental and emotional response to the circumstances of life."[1] The Greek word *phroneo* expands this definition. It means "to give one's mind to,[2] set one's mind on, a way of thinking."[3] The word expresses not merely an activity of the intellect, but also a movement of the will; it is both interest and decision at the same time. So the meaning extends to the idea of "taking sides with someone or something."[4]

According to Chuck Swindoll, we should "move our will" and "take sides" with gratitude. He writes:

> Words can never adequately convey the incredible impact of our attitude toward life. The longer I live the more convinced I become that life is 10 percent what happens to us and 90 percent how we respond to it. This may shock you. But I believe the single most significant decision I can make on a day-to-day basis is my choice of attitude.[5]

I think he's on to something.

AN ATTITUDE OF GRATITUDE

Thankfulness is a major theme in the Bible. Every morning the Levites, who took part in the temple worship, were to stand to thank and praise the Lord (see 1 Chronicles 1). The Psalms encourage us over thirty-five times to give thanks to God, and

Paul expresses thanksgiving to God eighteen times in his letters in the New Testament. There are over 140 references to giving thanks in the Bible. From cover to cover, God's Word calls us to thankfulness, "Be a thankful people, let it become such a part of your being that you overflow with thankfulness!" (Colossians 2:7, AUTHOR'S PARAPHRASE). "Therefore as you have received Christ Jesus the Lord, so walk in Him, having been firmly rooted and now being built up in Him and established in your faith, just as you were instructed, and overflowing with gratitude" (Colossians 2:6-7). As Christians we are to live by faith and to overflow with gratitude. These are hallmarks of our walk. One Bible teacher went so far as to say that the level of our thankfulness is directly related to our level of spirituality.[6]

We are commanded to be thankful, but there is another reason to pursue an attitude of gratitude: It is how we are to come into the presence of the Lord.

> Enter His gates with thanksgiving
> And His courts with praise.
> Give thanks to Him, bless His name.
> (Psalm 100:4)

Let me ask you a question. When you repeat yourself over and over to your children, why do you do it? Because you think they aren't hearing. They're saying "yeah" and nodding their heads, but you know your words aren't penetrating, so you keep repeating yourself as they look at you and sigh, "Oh, Mom, really . . . yeah, yeah, yeah." I believe that God repeats himself twice in Psalm 100 because we, like little children, don't always hear what He says to us. Two times He says, "Be thankful." Two times He says, "Be filled with praise." It is very important to God that we enter His presence with grateful hearts, overflowing with thanksgiving. Is this how we come to Him?

Sadly, many of us do not come with an attitude of gratitude, but with an attitude of grumbling.

AN ATTITUDE OF GRUMBLING

This was the Israelite's problem. God had just displayed His awe-some power by supernaturally rescuing them from the terror of the Egyptian army. He had parted the Red Sea, allowing the Israelites to walk across unscathed. Can you begin to imagine what it was like to experience God's power in this way? To their left and to their right the sea waters rose like a skyscraper over them, yet the walls of water were held back by the right hand of their Almighty God. As God's people stood on solid ground on the other side of the Red Sea, they watched the towers of water cascade down, drowning the well-equipped Egyptian army. Filled with gratitude, Miriam and the women raised their tambourines and danced while the sons of Israel sang a glorious song of deliverance.

> I will sing to the LORD, for He is highly exalted;
> the horse and its rider He has hurled into the sea.
> The LORD is my strength and song. . . . Who is
> like You, majestic in holiness, awesome in praises,
> working wonders? (Exodus 15:1,11)

Would you believe that just three days after rejoicing before the Lord for His miraculous deliverance, the Israelites began to grumble? Just three days later! They grumbled because they were thirsty (see 15:24). They grumbled because they were hungry (see 16:2-3). They grumbled about Moses — the one who had led them out of Egypt and across the Red Sea safely (see 17:3), but Moses said their complaints were against the Lord rather than him (see 16:8).

I read about the Israelite's groaning and whining after their amazing deliverance and think, *How could they forget so easily? Had God not shown them His incredible power? Could the God who parted the Red Sea not provide drinking water in the desert for two million Jews?* Yet, I'm a lot like the Israelites. When trials come and I experience emotional hunger and thirst, I too forget God's provision and move from an attitude of gratitude to an attitude of grumbling.

Do all peoples grumble and whine? No. Elisabeth Elliot was surprised to discover that the children of the Auca Indians she worked with in South America never grumbled or complained. She believes that these children didn't grumble because they had not been taught to grumble. They had never heard their parents grumbling.

I wonder, what have my children learned from me? What have your children learned from you? If you had two baskets on the counter in your kitchen, one called your Grumbling Basket and the other called your Gratitude Basket, at the end of the day, which one would be filled? The day my Christmas tree toppled, my Grumbling Basket would have been filled to overflowing. But this isn't who I want to be. I don't think it is who you want to be either.

Grumbling and complaining both contain the element of fault-finding. When we complain we make a charge or an accusation. Many times our fault-finding, like the Israelites, is with God. When we grumble, we make mental or verbal charges against Him. Thanksgiving, on the other hand, always involves mental or verbal praise to God.

There is always something in life for us to grumble about, as reflected in the following examples of Murphy's Law:

- Nothing is as easy as it looks. Everything takes longer than you think. If anything can go wrong it will.
- The chance of the bread falling with the peanut butter-and-jelly side down is directly proportional to the cost of the carpet.
- No matter how long or hard you shop for an item, after you've bought it, it will be on sale somewhere cheaper.
- The other line always moves faster.
- Inside every large problem is a series of small problems struggling to get out.
- You will remember that you forgot to take out the trash when the garbage truck is two doors away.[7]

Yes, there is always something to grumble about. Will we have an attitude of gratitude or an attitude of grumbling? Consider what author Hannah Whitall Smith observed about gratitude and grumbling: "The soul that gives thanks can find comfort in everything; the soul that complains can find comfort in nothing."

Even more important, consider what God says about our hearts. What kind of attitude does He want us to have? Let's take a look.

A HEART THAT REMEMBERS GOD'S BENEFITS

Ten men from the most pitiful element of society came to Jesus for healing. They had a feared disease: leprosy. Lepers were outcasts from society, estranged from their families, hidden away in caves, their grotesque deformities swaddled in rags. Their physical and emotional misery was beyond description. We find the tender story of these ten lepers in Luke 17:11-19.

> Jesus was walking past their village, and these ten tragic men stood at a distance, crying out to him, "Jesus, Master, have mercy on us!" Jesus looked on their deep physical and emotional pain and said, "Go show yourselves to the priests." And as they went, they were cleansed of their leprosy. One of them, when he saw that he was healed, came back to Jesus, shouting, "Praise God!" He fell to the ground at Jesus' feet, thanking him (over and over) for what he had done. This man was a Samaritan. Jesus asked, "Didn't I heal ten men? Where are other nine? Has no one returned to give glory to God except this foreigner?" (AUTHOR'S PARAPHRASE)

I BOW MY ATTITUDE   133

What do we learn from this story? That Jesus heals! We also learn that when we get what we want, we, like the nine lepers, can easily take credit and go on our own merry way, forgetting to give thanks to God. Jerry Bridges has this to say about our attitude:

> We pray for God's intervention in our lives, then congratulate ourselves rather than God for the results. Some years ago when one of the American lunar missions was in serious trouble, the American people were asked to pray for the safe return of the astronauts. When they were safely back on earth, credit was given to the technological achievements and skill of the American space industry. No thanks or credit was publicly given to God.[8]

In addition to illustrating our tendency to forget to be thankful, the story of the ten lepers demonstrates another important point: Jesus equates giving thanks with giving glory to God. To Him, giving thanks is a BIG deal!

I wonder, would I have been the one to return and thank Jesus over and over, or would I have had a forgetful heart? How about you? Psalm 103:2 says, "Bless the LORD, O my soul, and forget none of His benefits." I want to be one who remembers God's benefits. I want to have a heart of gratitude. What about you?

A HEART THAT OFFERS A SACRIFICE OF PRAISE

It is hard to remember to be grateful, but it's even more difficult to offer thanksgiving when to do so demands sacrifice. Yet, this is what God asks of us.

> Through Him then, let us continually offer up a
> sacrifice of praise to God, that is, the fruit of lips
> that give thanks to His name. (Hebrews 13:15)

Three words jump out at me from this verse:

1. *Continually.* This means over and over — all the time, whether I feel like it or not.
2. *Sacrifice.* This involves burning, which means it will hurt.
3. *Thanks.* I am to give thanks to God over and over for things that hurt and are anything but pleasant.

Obviously, I can't do these things . . . but there are two other words, the most important words in the verse — *through Him.* Through Him, and only through Him, can I continually offer up a sacrifice of praise to God. I love Matthew Henry's commentary on the Bible, but most of all I love the author's heart for God. After being robbed, he wrote in his diary: "Let me be thankful. First, because I was never robbed before. Second, because although they took my wallet, they did not take my life. Third, because although they took my all, it was not much. Fourth, because it was I who was robbed, not I who robbed."[9] This precious attitude of gratitude shows me how far I have to go in offering my God a sacrifice of praise.

The psalmist David has been my example. He wrote, "I will praise God's name in song and glorify him with thanksgiving" (Psalm 69:30, NIV). "I will sacrifice a thank offering" (116:17, NIV). Notice how David expresses himself in such a decisive way.

"I will praise."

"I will glorify . . . with thanksgiving."

"I will sacrifice a thank offering."

David was a man of resolve who had developed a lifestyle of giving thanks. This could not have been easy. He often hid in caves, fearing for his life, yet a spirit of gratitude flowed from his lips.

The bottom line is this: Often, I don't want to praise God because it is easier, more natural, for me to grumble and complain. The sacrifice comes when I put to death my inclinations, when I kill my urge to whine. Then, after putting to death my natural tendency, I must call forth from deep within me the buried treasure of praise. This often requires great discipline and a truckload of emotional energy.

Recently, God allowed a very difficult situation in my life. Someone close to me deeply hurt me and my mind was filled with negative, debilitating thoughts about this person. It was as if my mind was on auto-pilot in whiny, grumbling gear. "God," I cried, "please show me how to shift into the right gear. I am stuck, stuck, stuck." Gently He reminded me of what I already knew, what I'd practiced and taught others for years. "Linda, a thankful spirit is the way out of the pit. The Holy Spirit, your Helper and Encourager, will shift the gear for you, but you must also do your part. Have you thanked me? I know you see nothing positive, but can you offer me a sacrifice of thanksgiving?"

So I began doing what I knew to do but wasn't doing. Each morning before I even put my feet on the floor, I lay in bed and meditated on Philippians 4:8.

> Finally, brethren, whatever is true, whatever is honorable, whatever is right, whatever is pure, whatever is lovely, whatever is of good repute, if there is any excellence and if anything worthy of praise, dwell on these things.

Then I talked to the wonderful Holy Spirit within me, and asked Him to encourage me. "Lord, remind me of the positive about this person who hurt me. I choose to set my mind today on their excellent and praiseworthy qualities."

Each evening before I drifted off to sleep, the Holy Spirit and I talked, "I need you to remind me of the positive, Precious

Encourager." And the Father, Son, and Spirit shifted my attitude and I began thanking God for EVERYTHING that came to my mind, everything about the difficult situation and about ALL of life.

While it's difficult to always offer a sacrifice of thanksgiving, when I do, the Holy One rejoices, and an attitude of gratitude fills my heart. The same is true when I give thanks in *all* things.

A HEART THAT GIVES THANKS IN ALL THINGS

One thing we can say about the Bible: There are a lot of hard but interesting statements found in its pages. For instance:

> And give thanks for everything to God the Father in the name of our Lord Jesus Christ. (Ephesians 5:20, NLT)

Here's another one:

> Do all things without grumbling or disputing; so that you will prove yourselves to be blameless and innocent, children of God above reproach in the midst of a crooked and perverse generation, among whom you appear as lights in the world. (Philippians 2:14-15)

Think on that last verse for a minute. It says that if you have an attitude of gratitude instead of an attitude of grumbling, people watching your life will find nothing to criticize. The next verse says your thankful spirit will make your life a bright shining light in this dark world. But, oh, it is hard not to complain and to give thanks in all things!

I can relate to Corrie ten Boom's not wanting to thank God for the horrible, creepy, crawly things in the concentration camp. Corrie and her sister, Betsy, had just been transferred to the worst German prison camp they had seen yet, Ravensbruck. On entering the barracks, they found them infested with fleas. That morning, their Bible reading in 1 Thessalonians had reminded them to rejoice always, pray constantly, and give thanks in all circumstances. Betsy told Corrie to stop and thank the Lord for every detail of their new living quarters. At first Corrie flatly refused to give thanks for the fleas, but Betsy persisted, and Corrie finally thanked God for the pesky, horrible fleas. During the months they spent at that camp, the sisters were surprised to find how openly they could hold Bible study and prayer meetings without interference from the guards. Many months passed before they learned the reason the guards would not enter the barracks — the fleas![10]

Sometimes God reveals to us the purpose for the fleas, other times He doesn't. This week I prayed with Shannon while she sobbed over her daughter's rebellious attitude. She told me, "Linda, I can't thank God that McKenna is walking away from Him. I know what the Bible says, give thanks in everything . . . but could God be in this?" I wept with my friend. We took this huge anxiety and lifted her precious McKenna to the only One strong enough to hold her, and we laid her at His feet. Then I heard Shannon whisper, *My Lord, I don't understand why I am to thank you for this, but I trust that you are going to work good out of this heartache. I offer you a sacrifice of thanksgiving. It hurts, Lord. Receive it as my worship.*

I pictured the Almighty God with His hands outstretched, welcoming this hurting mother's worship. Her attitude of thanksgiving was a sacrifice of praise to the One who is worthy.

I want to worship God with my attitude. Do you? Let's look at some ways to throw out the grumbling, whining, and complaining and usher in an attitude of gratitude.

COME, LET'S GET PRACTICAL

One woman wrote this about how she moves her mind and will from grumbling to gratitude.

- Reading the psalms always moves me toward gratitude. Sometimes I have to read a psalm three or four times before I agree with the psalmist in his gratitude.
- When alone in my car, I shout the precious promises of Christ until I stop grumbling.
- When I am really low and self-absorbed in my dismal swamp, I find a place to give, even if it's just taking a load of stuff to the Salvation Army or sending an encouraging email.

Here are some other suggestions for how you can cultivate a grateful heart:

1. *Make a thankful list or keep a thankful journal.* Each week have a Thanksgiving Day — not a day for turkey and trimmings but a day to quietly reflect on what you have to thank God for. You don't have to write a lot, one page will do. Let your mind free flow and make a list or write a paragraph. Just write.

Mary Anne, a precious woman I met when I spoke at Ft. Carson, wrote the following list of thanksgiving. Her husband was killed in Iraq a year ago.

God, I thank you for . . .

- Christ's grace, mercy, and love when walking through this valley of weeping.
- Carrying my burdens.
- Comforting me with strength and peace.
- Four and a half years of adventure, love, and intimacy with my soulmate.

❧ Entrusting me to have loved this amazing creature who had a heart for you.

❧ Glorifying yourself through my husband's death, and through my grief and brokenness.

❧ Giving your life for mine and living with you, just as Charlie is doing right now.

❧ Fulfilling your promises and being repetitive in reassuring me.

❧ Allowing me to feel the emotions of loving someone and being loved.

❧ Loving me and never giving up on me, even when the road ahead seems too long to travel alone.

How Mary Anne's grateful spirit must delight the Lord! Yours will too.

2. *Count your blessings.* Consider buying two special boxes: one black and one gold, and putting them in a place where you will see them every day. Read the following story daily, and ask God each time you see the black and gold boxes to help you remember to count your blessings!

> I have in my hands two boxes that God gave me
> to hold.
> He said, "Put all your sorrows in the black box,
> and all your joys in the gold."
> I heeded His words, and in the two boxes both
> my joys and sorrows I stored,
> but though the gold became heavier each day the
> black was as light as before.
> With curiosity, I opened the black, I wanted to
> find out why,
> and I saw, in the base of the box, a hole which my
> sorrow had fallen out by.

I showed the hole to God, and asked, "I wonder
   where my sorrows could be."
He smiled a gentle smile and said, "My child,
   they're all here with me."
I asked God why He gave me the boxes, why the
   gold, and the black with the hole?
"My child, the gold is for you to count your
   blessings,
the black is for you to let go."[11]

3. *Make a sign.* My wonderful daughter-in-law, Deirdre, had this
very special sign written in her kitchen to remind her of what was
important when her three boys, Finn, Ronan, and Aidan, were
ages four, two, and six months. Notice how many times she says
to give thanks. (Deirdre has a basket of gratitude on her kitchen
sink.)

> Respond with love, always. Read to Ronan....
> Give Finn space. Kiss and hug. Take more deep
> breaths. Relax and have fun. Get them out-
> doors as much as possible.... Be consistent....
> Praise. Praise. Praise. Give thanks every day....
> Encourage creativity and imagination. Keep them
> safe and get out of their way. Don't make their
> fun for them. Give out more treats. Show them
> life is a ball! Give thanks. Give more thanks. And
> Remember: Time is flying by. They will not always
> be this little.... ENJOY THEM NOW!!

4. *Wrap a gift and keep it by your bed* to remind yourself each morning to thank God for the gift of today ... to fill your mind with
thankfulness ... and each night to go over the day and thank God
for the gift of today. "This is the day which the LORD has made; [I
WILL] rejoice and be glad in it"(Psalm 118:24).

5. *Ask God for "thankful triggers."* Whenever Lorraine has to wait for the train to pass (this happens frequently, as she lives by a train track) she uses this time to thank God. The passing train is her "thankful trigger." Every time I pass Elise's church on the freeway, I offer thanks for her. Alexa passes her children's school several times a day, and each time she thanks God for something positive about her children.

As you put these things into practice, you will begin growing in gratitude.

GROWING IN GRATITUDE

The Father calls your attitude of gratitude worship. When you choose to not give in to whining but instead to offer a sacrifice of thanksgiving, the God of the universe rejoices! And you? You grow in grace. You grow toward that wonderful place Paul calls "overflowing with gratitude." Have you ever known a woman with a truly thankful heart? I hope so. She is a joy to everyone around her and a delight to her God.

If I close my eyes I can see an old woman who overflows with thanksgiving. She has a beautiful smile and a contagious laugh. Her strength is drawn from the River of Living Water, and she whispers to her Lord with a confident intimacy that entices me. An attitude of gratitude flows over her because she has developed a lifestyle of giving thanks in everything — it has become a part of her very nature. She no longer has to tell herself, "Remember to be thankful." Her thankful spirit is a byproduct of years of walking with her God. This is the woman I want to become.

Who do you want to become? Will you come with me for a short walk? Will you walk around your attitude — look at it from all sides? I know. Some of it isn't pleasant to look on — some even smells not-so-sweet. But keep looking. I want you to see beyond the natural. I want you to see what God sees. Your attitude can become worship! That grumbling, negative, complaining spirit can be lifted and transformed and turned into a spirit that will minister unto the Lord of the universe. Amazing.

Now visualize the new you, with your Gratitude Basket over your arm, walking up the steps to the throne of God. The Holy One smiles and gently says, "My daughter, I see you brought me the offering of your gratitude. I love that! Show me what's in your basket." You pull out your thankful list, and as you pull, you're surprised at how it's grown. Your list is growing, and you are growing. Gratitude is becoming a part of you!

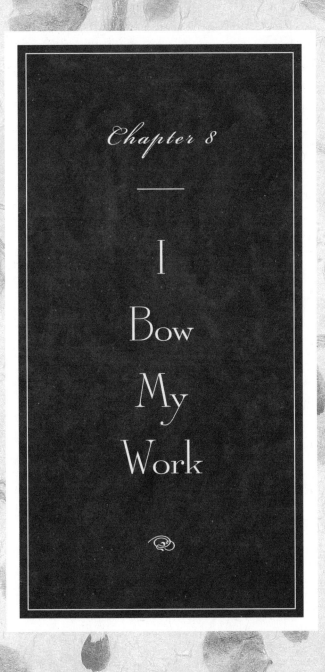

Chapter 8

—

I

Bow

My

Work

I Bow My Work

Come let us worship and bow down,

Let us bow our work in worship before God.

PSALM 95:6, AUTHOR'S PARAPHRASE

I am so frustrated with my computer that I am ready to give up, scream, and vow never to write again. I have been working for five hours, and it looks as if I have lost all my work. I hate computers. I don't want to see one again. If I wouldn't look immature and unchristian, I would throw my computer out the window.

All of us have throw-the-computer-out-the-window days. Days when our work makes us want to scream, sob, sigh, shout, and sniffle. The very word *work* can conjure up distasteful images.

Kelly:

> I came home from a stressful day at the clinic to
> a three-year-old who was yelling his head off. I'd
> felt like screaming all day, and I just shut myself
> in our bedroom and out-screamed my son. The
> sad thing is, it felt good.

Jana:

> I have a master's degree in international business,
> and the only job I can find is as a sales clerk in a
> clothing store.

Brittany:

If I have to clean up one more child's vomit, I'm going to throw up — all over everyone else. Motherhood is definitely not what I signed up for.

Tammy:

My job as a customer sales rep is so stressful, but I need it because my husband is out of work. Why does work have to be so agonizingly hard?

Kaylie:

I don't want to prepare this fancy meal. I don't want to prepare the guest room. I'm tired of preparing for people. I want to be alone with a good book, popcorn, and a Diet Coke. Please, God, NO WORK.

If you, like me, feel stressed to the max with too many jobs, you can identify with these women. Work can be exhausting, frustrating, discouraging, disappointing, beyond boring, and just plain hard. But in reality, our work is not our problem. Our problem is our perspective. I recently saw this truth vividly illustrated by a flight attendant.

A HIGHER VIEW

Bleary-eyed, I sat at Gate 1, waiting for my flight. It was 6 a.m. Slumped in seats around me were other zombie-like commuters wondering what had possessed them to schedule this early morning departure. I had asked myself this question many times since my alarm clock had blared at 4 a.m.

Hearing vibrant laughter, I looked up, wondering, *Who laughs at 6 a.m.?* A flight attendant, the source of the laughter, was walking through the security area, her warmth touching each person she encountered. Later, on the plane, this caring angel sat on an armrest and listened to the life story of a man, paralyzed from birth. Up and down the aisle she moved, smiling, helping, and handing out roses. I asked Bea where she had found the roses, and she said, "They were given to me, and I wanted to share them."

Perhaps you think that Bea's life reads like the script of *It's a Wonderful Life*. Not so. Her life could be called *It's a Miserable Life*. Talking with her, I learned that she was a single mom whose son had just been released from prison. Some flight attendants go through the motions of serving. Bea told me she loved the Lord Jesus, and it was obvious that she served from her heart because her heart belonged to the Creator. Bea's work is her worship.

She has a higher view of her work. This is what I need. It is what you need. Bea is a common woman living an uncommon life. She has learned what Christians centuries ago knew:

Laborare est orare; orare est laborare.

Once prominently displayed in places of work, this Latin saying translated into English means, "To work is to worship; to worship is to work."[1] Stop for a moment and digest this thought. Then ask yourself: Do I see my work as worship? Paul's words to the Colossians indicate we should. "Whatever you do in word or deed, do all in the name of the Lord Jesus" (Colossians 3:17). How do you see your work? The pile of laundry, the stack of ungraded papers, the document you need to write, the patients you need to see? No matter your work, do you see it as worship? Does your work have *Laborare est orare* written over it?[2]

What is your work? Crunching numbers in an office cubicle? Dealing with angry customers? Organizing unreliable volunteers? Teaching thankless teens? Counseling women? Raising children? Delivering mail? Delivering food? Delivering babies? Have you sometimes viewed your work as trivial or insignificant? Do you feel that you are biding time changing diapers or ink cartridges until your real dream job comes along?

The apostle Paul said your *life* is to be lifted as an offering, which is your spiritual act of worship (see Romans 12:1), and an important part of your *life* and what makes up you is your *work*.

How might our feelings about work change if we grasped the truth that our work can be worship? Think what it would be like in a carpool on Monday morning if the driver greeted everybody with, "Good morning! Here we go to worship." Just think what it would be like if a mother began each morning with the prayer, *Lord, let each task . . . diaper changes, preparing meals, washing clothes, answering my two-year-old's endless questions . . . be done as an act of worship to you.* Just think what life would be like if every teacher, nurse, computer programmer, lawyer, doctor, and plumber said as they left for work, "I'm off to worship!" If we could live, "My work is worship, my worship is work," it would transform our work — and us!

Can you actually live your work as an act of worship? *Yes!* Can your work move from being frustrating to being fulfilling? *Yes!* You can begin to move to this place by changing how you think about your work, particularly when it comes to how you answer these three key questions:

1. How do I define success?

2. Do I see my work as significant?

3. Do I see some work as more sacred than other work?

Let's explore each of these.

How Do I Define Success?

If you say you've never asked this question, I don't think you are being honest. I have asked it many times. I asked it when I was home with three children under four, and the days were a blur of sameness. I asked it daily when I was a missionary trying to relate to the Austrian culture, traveling by subway to learn German, and winning the award for dropping German classes because my children got the chicken pox and then head lice (very gross). I did not think I was a success at learning German or relating to the culture (or getting rid of lice).

How does the world define success when it comes to our work? Primarily by our title, salary, and level of responsibility. This makes it difficult for moms at home to feel respected and valued. I was privileged to be a stay-at-home mom of four children with lots of responsibility and no paycheck ☺. I would not have traded the job for any other, but there were days when I had a hard time defining success. Certainly the children did not thank me or give me progress reports on the job I was doing.

Then one day I came upon God's definition of success, and it changed how I viewed my work.

> Whatever you do, do your work heartily, as for the Lord rather than for men, knowing that from the Lord you will receive the reward of the inheritance. It is the Lord Christ whom you serve. (Colossians 3:23-24)

Oh, isn't this passage wonderful? It gives us a clear definition of success. Listen to how *The Message* renders these verses: "Do your best. Work from the heart for your real Master, for God, confident that you'll get paid in full when you come into your inheritance. Keep in mind always that the ultimate Master you're serving is Christ." And the *Amplified Bible* says, "Whatever may be your task, work at it heartily (from the soul) . . ."

How does Scripture define success? A woman is successful if she:

* Does her work for God, the One for whom she works.
* Does her work heartily, from her heart and from her soul.
* Works to receive a reward, not a temporary reward such as money, but an eternal reward, which will last forever.

I told you about Bea, the flight attendant who inspired me with her attitude. I want to tell you about another inspiring worker, a flagman. During a frustrating commute one Monday morning, a driver observed a traffic flagman dancing as he performed his job. Seemingly oblivious to the July sun, blaring horns, and impatient commuters, the man swung his orange flags in wide, graceful arcs, and called out friendly greetings to passing motorists. Astounded by the joy this man exhibited in what most would consider a boring job, the driver rolled down the car window and asked the man how he could be so enthusiastic.

"I'm happy because I'm not working for the man," he shouted back. "I'm a flagman for Jesus."[3]

Work done as work is a flight attendant who grudgingly passes out drinks or a flagman who brusquely directs cars down a road. Work done as worship is a flight attendant who says a prayer for each person who receives the drink she offers, or a dancing flagman who says, "I'm directing traffic for Jesus."

I am humbled by the flagman. Whatever our job, may we become flagwomen for Jesus.

We've looked at what defines success; now let's explore what gives significance to our work.

DO I SEE MY WORK AS SIGNIFICANT?

While speaking at a women's group recently, I asked, "Do you often feel the work you do is insignificant?" Nearly all raised their hands. When I asked why, here are some of the reasons the women gave.

My work feels insignificant because:

- I am not paid much for what I do.
- My work is behind-the-scenes, while the people I work for are in the spotlight.
- I work as a wife and mother and wonder if it is enough to do.
- I don't see immediate results from what I do.
- I work in a secular environment where I can't talk about God so I don't feel what I am doing has much eternal impact.
- I don't have a fancy, impressive title.
- When I tell people what I do, they have no interest and quickly change the subject.

Fortunately, significance in God's economy looks very different from in ours. Look with me in the gospel of Mark, where we read of a man who was responsible for the ordinary task of preparing the room for the Last Supper. The disciples were ready to go shopping, put on their aprons, and prepare a Passover meal. But Jesus told them someone had already done so.

> "Go into the city, and a man will meet you carrying a pitcher of water; follow him; and wherever he enters, say to the owner of the house, 'The Teacher says, "Where is My guest room in which I may eat the Passover with My disciples?"' And he himself will show you a large upper room

furnished and ready; prepared for us there." The
disciples went out and came to the city, and found
it just as He had told them; and they prepared the
Passover. (Mark 14:13-16)

This unnamed man's work was a simple thing. A room.
Prepared. Made ready for the King. You, like me, have prepared
rooms for guests. It takes time and effort. This worker probably
beat the rugs, swept the floor, dusted, and polished. I'm sure he
made a trip to the well to draw fresh water so that the guests' feet
could be washed and their parched throats refreshed. Mundane
things . . . yet this simple preparation was important. Jesus knew
the work the man had accomplished; He knew how the man had
served Him. Some days you may feel like an "unnamed worker."
You wonder, *Who sees me? Who cares what I do?* Just as Jesus saw and
cared about what this man had done, He sees and values all that
you do when you do it for Him.

Down through the centuries, Christians have loved *Practicing
the Presence of God.* In this treasured volume, we learn how to worship with our work, even ordinary work. Brother Lawrence's little
book is one of my favorites. Perhaps you know his name. But do you
know the name of M. Beaufort? I didn't, but without him I would
not have the joy of continually reading and rereading *Practicing the
Presence of God.* After Brother Lawrence's death, M. Beaufort, grand
vicar of M. de Chalons, worked at compiling the conversations and
letters that became the precious record of Brother Lawrence's walk
in God's presence. Yet whose name is remembered? M. Beaufort's
or Brother Lawrence's? Was M. Beaufort's work significant? Was it
less or more significant than the work of Brother Lawrence? Good
questions to ponder. (We'll talk more about Brother Lawrence in
chapter 12.)

Another name you probably know is Oswald Chambers.
Many hundreds of thousands have drawn nearer to God through
his wonderful devotional, *My Utmost for His Highest.* Chambers died

unexpectedly at age forty-two, and his dear wife, Biddy, spent the rest of her life compiling his scattered notes into the daily devotional. Few know her name, few know of her devoted labors, but without Biddy Chambers, the world would not have known Oswald Chambers and been blessed and edified by *My Utmost for His Highest.* Whose work was of greater significance? Oswald Chambers, whose name is known, or Biddy Chambers, who is relatively unknown? An interesting question.

What about a woman whose mind has been shattered? Who has no memory? What work can she do? I learned just how significant a broken life can be through Mae. After meeting her, I wrote in my journal:

> I've spent many hours this week in a convalescent home that smells mildly of urine. Sometimes more than mildly. Most would say it is a depressing place. Half the people stare blankly, many cannot speak. Those, like my stepfather, who are in this place for physical therapy after surgery beg to go home. People of sound mind run for the exit because death stalks here. Yet God has stationed a light in this darkness. Her name is Mae. She is old and bent. Her hair is fuzzy and sticks out. Her speech slurs. Alzheimer's has turned her once sharp mind hazy.
>
> As I prayed over Mae, she said, "Marlene (she never gets my name right), God has me here to be a light." On days she can read, Mae reads the Bible to Rosemary. She speaks slurred words of encouragement to James. For six years Mae has lived in this place as a light. She wept as I asked the Father to shine through His precious lighthouse named Mae. Mae worships her God through her work.

As I think about M. Beaufort, Biddy Chambers, and dear Mae, I am reminded of Paul's words in 1 Corinthians 4:2: "It is required of Linda and other Christian women that they be found faithful" (AUTHOR'S PARAPHRASE). God's standard differs from ours. We feel that we must achieve to feel significant, but God says, "Be faithful in your work, my daughter, and you will find significance in my sight."

We've looked at what defines success for us and what gives significance to our work. We have one more question to explore.

DO I SEE SOME WORK AS MORE SACRED THAN OTHER WORK?

Something has gotten twisted in our modern minds. We look at our life and divide it into two compartments. We place all the "spiritual" in one compartment and all the "secular" in another. Spiritual is going to church, teaching Sunday school, praying, or cooking a meal for someone in our Bible study. Secular is the daily routine of making beds, cooking a meal for our family, changing diaper number six for the day, or cleaning up yet one more glass of spilled milk — or going to the office, school, factory, or clothing store. But, my friends, this perspective is unbiblical.

Sue Kline, editor of *Discipleship Journal* magazine (a very spiritual-sounding job), recalls spending a morning in a store, looking for her favorite sandals. A young man sporting numerous tattoos, a goatee, and an in-your-face T-shirt waited on her. "I was treated like royalty by a man who loved his work. Nothing in my size? Nothing in the style I wanted? No problem. With cheerfulness, respect, and tenacity, he pursued the elusive sandals right to the manufacturer."

Most would say that there was nothing sacred or spiritual about the "work" of the tattooed salesman. Sue has a different perspective. She believes work becomes sacred based on how we perform it. The helpful clerk displayed kindness, joy, patience, diligence, and a desire to serve — all qualities of Christlikeness. This encounter made Sue realize that even though she works for a Christian magazine, she has sometimes displayed impatience with a colleague, complained about a writer who doesn't follow directions, and participated in gossip — all unChristlike qualities. She was forced to ask, "Which work was secular and which was spiritual?"[4] Good question.

On Mondays and Tuesdays Kim works ten-hour days as a social worker at a hospital. The other five days of the week she is home with three boys, ages three, five, and seven. On Sundays Kim is on the worship team at church, using her beautiful voice to lead worshippers in singing. How would you rate Kim's work? Is it more Christlike to minister to a hurting woman in the hospital than to stop fights between little boys? Are Kim's actions more spiritual when she lifts her hands in worship than when she lifts one of her boys into her arms? Is leading worship of higher value than washing muddy clothes or cleaning a toilet where little boys have missed the mark?

I think Mother Teresa would have said that *everything* Kim does is "spiritual work." When Mother Teresa was asked what worship meant to her, her response was a beautiful portrait of worshipping with our work. She said that when she helped an orphan in the street, when she gave a cup of cold water to a thirsty child, she was worshipping God. After all, didn't Jesus say, "Whatever you did for one of the least of these brothers of mine, you did for me"?[5]

Each of your small moments of work, bowed before God, not only gives joy to others, but is also counted as worship to the Holy One. He sees, He is ministered to. Every drop of water given in His name, every word typed on the computer, every patient served, every meal prepared, every sick child held . . . all are acts of worship. Elaine understands this. Over the sink in her kitchen is a plaque that reads, "Divine Services Held Here 3x a Day."

We sometimes forgot that for the first thirty years of His

life the Lord Jesus was a laborer, a carpenter. He pounded nails, carried boards, built things out of wood. Creating out of wood was His preparation for ministry. The Lord makes it clear that we should not make a distinction between spiritual and secular. The two flow together. We see this clearly in the making of the Tabernacle. I love the picture in Exodus 35:25-26. It was as if God was calling, "Come, my daughters, all you who can sew or spin. You have a unique skill that I can use. Come dear women whose hearts have been stirred with a skill." What a beautiful picture of the gifts God gives to His women!

When we divide the sacred from the secular, we can wrongly think that God gives the Holy Spirit for spiritual work, such as preaching, teaching, counseling, or healing, but not for secular work. But this is not true. The Bible says, "The LORD has filled Bezalel with the Spirit of God, giving him great wisdom, ability, and expertise in all kinds of crafts" (Exodus 35:31, NLT). Here we see that the Spirit was given in order to help this man create beauty through crafts, such as sewing, spinning, sculpting, and carving. In God's eyes, there is no division between the sacred and the secular. He is the Creator of all. ALL your work is important to Him! He is in all, over all, and longs for you to glorify Him in all . . . for you to lift up your work as worship to Him.

Is this way of thinking about your work new for you? Do you see that all of work is spiritual? Do you agree with God's view of successful work? A. W. Tozer was right when he said, "We're here to be worshipers first and workers only second. . . . The work done by a worshiper will have eternity in it."[6]

At the end of my life I want to be able to say what the Lord Jesus said: "I have brought you glory on earth by completing the work you gave me to do" (John 17:4, NIV). Some days my work is to sit at the computer and write. Other days it is to stand in front of groups of women and teach God's Word. Some days it is to cook and clean for guests, other days to hold a sobbing woman who has suffered sexual abuse and to pray over her. Other days I garden, sit on planes, paint a room, or watch a friend's children. All of this is spiritual work. Every facet of my work can be as worship as I bow it to the One I love, as I do each task to the best of my ability so that He might be glorified. I want each day of the rest of my life to say to God, "I offer all my work today to you as an act of worship." As you look at the many facets of your work, I pray that you too long to say, "Lord, I want to offer my work today to you as an act of worship."

Now let's look at how you can take some steps to begin to worship God with your work.

Come, Let's Get Practical

1. *Memorize, meditate, and personalize back to God Colossians 3:23-24.* (I know you're groaning — memorization is hard work but you can do it!) Take these precious verses and make them a part of you, then talk to your Father about them as you begin your day of work:

> Whatever you do, do your work heartily, as for
> the Lord rather than for men, knowing that from
> the Lord you will receive the reward of the inheri-
> tance. It is the Lord Christ whom you serve.

Here's how two women I know prayed these verses in their own words:

> *Father, I need help today with these kids. I want to do my work as a mom with all my soul — I want to do it for you, Lord. No one sees what I do all day, but you do and I know my reward comes from you. Let me remember that today. I want my work as a mom today to be as worship to you because I love you.*

Lord, as I drive to work today, my to-do list is so long I feel dis-couraged before I even walk in the door. But I'm here before you to say I want to work from my heart for you, God. You are the One I am truly working to please and my lasting reward comes from you. Please empower me so I can serve you well.

Burn these verses on your heart and mind. Then burn this concept about worship deep within you.

2. *Make a plaque for your desk or wherever you do your work that says,* Laborare est Orare. Orare est Laborare. I have two little plaques with this reminder that to work is to worship. One sits on my desk, and every day when I see it I remember that my work at my computer can be worship to my God. The second plaque sits on the window-sill by my kitchen sink. When I see it, I am reminded that every veggie chopped, each meal prepared, and every pot scrubbed can become worship.

I find dwelling on this Latin message that has encouraged Christians for centuries prompts me to lift prayers more fre-quently about:

- ❧ My work.
- ❧ My attitude about my work.
- ❧ My faithfulness in doing my work.

What is worship? It is taking the part of my life called work and placing it on the altar as my offering to my God because I love Him. This is my spiritual act of worship. *Laborare est Orare. Orare est Laborare.* Work is worship. Worship is work. Do you get it? Please say "yes!" This is important! Your work today can be as worship to the Holy One!

Will you make a choice to offer your work to God as an act of worship? Will you pray this beautiful poem titled *Laborare Est Orare*.

> *Laborare Est Orare*
> "Laborare est orare,"
> Sang a monk of ancient time;
> Sang it at his early matin,
> Sang it at the vesper chime.
>
> "Work is worship;"
> God, my brothers,
> Takes our toils for homage sweet
> And accepts as signs of worship
> Well worn hands and wearied feet.
>
> "Laborare est orare,"
> Watchword of the old divine,
> Let us take it for our motto
> Serving in this later time.
>
> Work is worship; toil! Is sacred:
> Let this thought our zeal inspire,
> Every deed done well and bravely
> Burns with sacrificial fire.
>   — Thomas W. Hanford[7]

A Prayer for Those Who Work Outside the Home

Lord Jesus, as I enter this workplace,
I bring your presence with me.
I speak your peace, your grace, and your perfect order into
   the atmosphere of this office.
I acknowledge your lordship over all that will be spoken,
   thought, decided, and accomplished within these walls.
Lord Jesus, I thank you for the gifts you have deposited in
   me.
I do not take them lightly, but commit to using them responsi-
   bly and well.
Give me a fresh supply of truth and beauty on which to draw
   as I do my job.
Anoint my creativity, my ideas, my energy, so that even my
   smallest task may bring you honor.
Lord, when I am confused, guide me. When I am weary, ener-
   gize me.
Lord, when I am burned out, infuse me with the light of your
   Holy Spirit.
May the work that I do and the way I do it, bring hope, life, and
   courage to all that I come in contact with today.
And, oh Lord, even in this days most stressful moment, may I
   rest in you.
In the mighty name that is above all names,
In the Matchless Name of my Lord and Savior Jesus I pray,
Amen.[8]

Chapter 9

—

I

Bow

My

Times of

Waiting

Chapter 9

I Bow My Times of Waiting

Come let us worship and bow down,

Let us bow our timeline in worship to God.

PSALM 95:6, AUTHOR'S PARAPHRASE

I sat at the computer, drummed my fingers impatiently, and stared with irritation at the tiny hourglass. How long was this going to take? The hourglass told me to keep waiting . . . seven, eight, nine . . . good grief, it had been at least ten seconds! Why hadn't the important email from Europe popped up on my screen yet?

As I looked at myself, I thought, *Get a grip, Linda. How is it that you have grown so impatient? Here you are irritated and agitated about a ten-second wait. When you lived in Europe twenty years ago, it took over a week to receive a letter from your college freshman in the States. Now you're in finger-drumming mode over a few seconds, wait. How pathetic.*

I know that I'm not alone in wanting instant everything. Many of us are impatient to the max. Our electronic age breeds impatience. It is not the same world it was twenty years ago. Then, we waited for food to cook and mail to arrive. Now it's drive-through, microwave meals, and instant messaging. And we hate waiting. We hate waiting for anything.

But I personally think the hardest waiting is waiting on God. God often makes no sense in how He operates His world. Will the waiting be two weeks, two years, or a lifetime? How much anguish will the waiting hold? We never know, which is why it is so agonizing.

Sometimes God can be quick. He's answered some of my

163

prayers with lightning speed, and I LOVE IT, love it, love it when He works like that. But this is not the norm for how He works in my life, or yours, or anyone's I know. Scripture reveals God as having deliberate timing, often a slow timing. The Israelites waited 430 years to leave Egypt. God could have delivered them after 430 days, but Exodus tells us that "It was on the last day of the 430th year . . . this night the LORD kept his promise to bring his people out from the land of Egypt" (Exodus 12:41-42, NLT). God wrote in His Palm Pilot that day number 365 of the 430th year was to be the Day of Deliverance. Why did He wait so many years? I'm sure it seemed like an eternity to the ones forced to make bricks by their Egyptian slave drivers. God's glorious power was available to bring the Israelites out of Egypt every minute of those 430 years. I certainly don't understand why He waited, and I'm sure the Israelites felt God was not going to answer their prayers for deliverance.

God's timing is a confusing mystery. It was a mystery to the Israelites. It was also a mystery to Joseph. Sold into slavery by his brothers, then falsely accused by his boss's wife, Joseph landed in prison. One day I added up the years this man spent in a pit and in prison (when he was innocent), waiting on God to clear his name. Thirteen years! As we quickly turn the pages of our Bibles, we often overlook the long wait. Joseph suffered deeply while waiting for his day of deliverance.

Perhaps you are currently in the agony of waiting. Are you waiting for a child? A mate? A husband to turn from sin? A job? Restored health? Healing, wholeness, forgiveness, or a new beginning? Are you waiting for love, friendship, or reconciliation with your family? You may feel like screaming, "God, I just don't get you! Why, why, why do you make people who love you wait? Why do you make people you say you love wait in agony for so long?"

I'm watching several friends wait for healing from sexual abuse. Two other friends are waiting for teens to wake up from their rebellious ways and return to the families who love them. I have friends who are waiting for healing from intense emotional pain. Then there is Valerie, who is waiting to be healed of deep physical pain. Let me tell you her story.

At age forty-two Valerie was happily married, the mom of four, and training for her fifth marathon. Within weeks her life drastically changed. Severe abdominal pain took her from running twenty-six miles to not being able to walk down the stairs. For the last two of the past five pain-filled years, she had to wear maternity clothes because of the swelling in her abdomen. Her days were spent going from doctor to doctor — from the Mayo Clinic to Stanford Medical Center. Finally, her doctors put a shunt in her liver, and for two weeks she was out of maternity clothes and in her size two jeans. Her stomach was once again flat. She'd been healed! Oh, how we praised and thanked God! But then the swelling returned, and the doctors said, "We just don't know . . ."

As I write this, Valerie is back in maternity clothes. (It's been over 600 days now.) The shunt is still in her liver, but the doctors don't know what to do. So, this former marathoner waits. She waits to have the strength to do something mundane, such as take out the trash. She waits to do something fun, like hike with her four children or belay the ropes for her rock-climbing daughters, who are ranked nationally in this sport. But a mom can't be involved in sports when she can't even take out the garbage. So this former marathoner sits in her maternity clothes and waits . . . and waits . . .

As a missionary, I've known people on three different continents. Guess what? Aversion to waiting is not just a North American trait, it is a universal trait. I've yet to meet a woman in any country who says, "I love being in the place where I have no idea what God is doing." Now this person may exist somewhere — perhaps you are this elusive woman — but I think for most of us, waiting is excruciating agony.

People handle waiting in various ways. Let's look in God's Word at three biblical characters and how they handled waiting. We will

see Sarah, who got tired and gave up; Peter, who got mad and got
in Jesus' way; and David, who got in God's face and got it right.

SARAH GOT IN GOD'S WAY

Sarah got tired of waiting and gave up. I can almost hear her
thoughts. *I know Abraham thinks he's heard from God. I believed it too . . . for
a while. It was a wonderful promise. I was to carry a baby in this weary, old body.
Imagine! A baby at my age! All my shame would crumble away and the joy, oh,
the joy! I would nurse a baby at my breast like other women, carry the little one
strapped on my back to the well. Oh, to feel his body moving against mine as I
walked up the hill to draw water. Night after night, year after year, I dreamed
only of this baby. Has any woman ever yearned with such deep longing? My body
has ached for this promised child. But so many years, so many dream-filled nights,
and no baby moved in my body. The ache was unbearable. God couldn't expect me
to continue waiting. How long is a woman supposed to wait for God when she is
old already? I tried, but finally I gave up. I came up with my own plan. I took my
maid Hagar and gave her to Abraham and told him to lie with her and get me a
child. If God couldn't do it the way He said He would, I'd get us a child — and
I did.*

Sarah got tired of waiting, gave up, and cooked up a scheme to
get what she desperately wanted. I would have labeled her a failure.
Yet God in His abundant grace lists her in the Faith Hall of Fame
(see Hebrews 11:11). Our God is a forgiving and remarkable God.
All of us are a mixture of faith and unbelief. But, oh, how I long
to bow before God's timeline and not give up. I can only imagine
how difficult it was for Sarah to wait for so many years for the
promised child she desperately desired. May we be women who
keep our eyes on the One who promises, may we bow before His
time schedule. He knows best and He loves us . . . even when we
don't understand.

Now let's look at how Peter reacted.

Peter Got in Jesus's Way

I have always identified with Peter, as I can be impulsive and am passionate by temperament. As I look over Peter's life, my heart saddens at his renunciation of Christ and rejoices when he risks his life to preach to thousands. As is the case for all of us, both triumph and failure filled the life of this fisherman whom Jesus deeply loved.

Peter had just been given the ultimate accolade by his Lord: "You are listening to the Father, Peter old boy. He is the One who revealed to you that I am the Christ. You are doing well, Peter. I am proud of you!" (Matthew 16:15-17, AUTHOR'S PARAPHRASE). Then, whamo! Six verses later, Jesus chastises Peter in the worst way possible. What Jesus says is horrible. In fact, He couldn't say anything worse. He calls Peter Satan! Here are the very words Jesus says to Peter: "Get behind Me, Satan! You are a stumbling block to Me; for you are not setting your mind on God's interests, but man's" (Matthew 16:23). What happened that caused Jesus to go from accolades to condemnation?

If you read Matthew 16:21-22, you will see that Jesus had begun to teach the disciples that He would be going to Jerusalem, where He would suffer and be killed, and that He would be raised from the dead on the third day. In essence, Jesus was telling those closest to Him that a time of waiting and suffering was coming. What did Peter do? "Peter [this is the Peter who had just said, 'You are the Christ!'] took Him aside and began to rebuke Him, saying, 'God forbid it, Lord! This shall never happen to You'" (Matthew 16:22).

Do you see what I see? Peter rebuked the Son of God. He didn't like the agenda Jesus had set forth and declared it in loud terms, forbidding Jesus to die, forbidding God's plan to happen. Peter tried to get in God's way. Peter refused to bow to God's agenda. Rarely do we see the Son of God angry, but He was livid with Peter.

Like Sarah and Peter, I am a reformed fixer. My old name was Linda Fixer Dillow. The sad thing was, I was really good at "fixing." God spent years chipping away gently and sometimes not-so-gently at my fixing tendencies. Often He did this through the agony of waiting. But, oh, how grateful I am that He has erased my middle name, blotted it out. I praise Him from the depths of my being. There is such freedom in resting in His agenda.

When do people get in God's way? This is something we must ponder. Here are some possible answers. We get in God's way when:

- *We only know part of the story.* Peter heard the word *killed* and missed the more important word, *resurrection.* The disciples were not expecting a resurrection. You would have thought Peter would have said, "Jesus, what do you mean by resurrection? I don't understand." When we are in a situation we don't understand, do we stop and ask, "Lord, what could your purposes be in the life of this person I love?"
- *We want to "fix a problem" because we care.* Problem is, when we start fixing someone's fix, we get in a fix ourselves. Fear says, "Get in there and fix it." Genuine love says, "Wait on God. Wait on His timing."
- *We want to "fix a problem" in order to protect ourselves.* It is so difficult to watch those we love suffer, and their pain causes us anguish. Sometimes it is easier for us to get into the midst of the mess (give money, for example) so that we won't suffer.

Ask any mother. It is easier to do *anything* than to just sit and wait on God on behalf of your children. Waiting on God when your child is in pain (even when that pain is self-induced) is agony beyond words. There is joy in being a lifegiver; it is a privilege. It is also a liability, because by trying to prevent pain in the lives of those we love, we can become a stumbling stone and block God's higher purposes. It is a difficult yet necessary lesson to learn. While God often calls us to put in place general rules of protection, He does not call us to categorically prevent the ones we love from hurting. *It is not our place to keep the ones we love from hurting.*

Peter was the disciple who declared that Jesus was "the Christ," but sometimes he got in God's way — as when he tried to make Jesus give up His calling to die for the sin of the world. Like Peter, sometimes we fail to wait on God's timing. We get in God's way too. But even though David struggled with God's timeline, he learned to wait on God.

DAVID WAITED ON GOD

David learned to wait on God in a beautiful and strong way. Like Sarah and Peter, David was a man of weakness and strength. He committed adultery and murder, but he confessed to both these sins and is called a man after God's own heart. We learn three things about how to wait from David: wait with courage, wait in hope, and bow to God's timeline.

1. Wait with Courage

> I would have despaired unless I had believed that
> I would see the goodness of the LORD in the land
> of the living.
> Wait for the LORD;
> Be strong and let your heart take courage;
> Yes, wait for the LORD. (Psalm 27:13-14)

Psalm 27 is one of the most beloved and quoted of the Psalms. Its message to the weary is: "Come, lift your weak heart, so full of despair." I know this fainting place where the heart droops, where the agony of waiting seems unbearable. These verses are not written by David the Shepherd or by David the King but by David the Warrior. The Warrior David rises up and calls out to his own heart, and then to ours, to be strong and of good courage. These words are a call to battle. Andrew Murray says they are frequently found in connection with some great and difficult enterprise and the utter insufficiency of all human strength. Is waiting on God a work so difficult, that such words are needed: "'Be strong, and let your heart take courage?'" Yes, indeed.[1]

Have you ever felt as if the waiting would never end, that you would not see the goodness of God until heaven? David had, and these words were his battle cry to persevere. It was godly self-talk of the best kind. "Get with it, David. Keep on waiting. God is faithful, even though you can't see it now. So be strong, old boy, and let your heart well up with courage. Come on, David, come on. Keep on keeping on waiting on the Lord!"

David waited with courage. He also waited with hope.

2. Wait in Hope

> Lead me by your truth and teach me,
> for you are the God who saves me.
> All day long I put my hope [I wait] in you. (Psalm
> 25:5, NLT)

While David waited, he hoped in his God. The Hebrew word for *wait* means to twist or stretch, and includes the idea of the tension of enduring.[2] It means to look forward with confident hope to that which is good and beneficial. The connotation evokes two images: connection and tension. The woman waiting on God in hope has a line directly connecting her with God. She and God are linked together, and her gaze follows the line right up to the throne of God and does not wander to the problems she is facing.

Visualize it like this: You, waiting on God, are at one end of a taut line connected to the One you are hoping in and waiting for, God Himself.

You  God

When I am in the throes of waiting, it helps me to quiet my heart, close my eyes, and see myself holding on to the stretched-out line. Even though I don't know how long I will wait, I am filled with hope, because I am not alone. God is connected to me, and my eyes gaze on Him, who is my hope. The line connecting me to God is not a limp line but a tension-filled line. Why? Because the possibility that my pain-filled days will stretch on with no end in sight creates physical tension. But remember, Waiting One, although waiting means tension, it also means connection, so keep your eyes on the Faithful One at the end of the taut line!

Hope and courage filled David's heart and allowed him to bow his timeline to God in worship.

3. Bow to God's Timeline

> But as for me, I trust in You, O Lord,
>   I say, "You are my God.
>   My times are in Your hand." (Psalm 31:14-15)

Of all the statements of faith recorded in Scripture, this is one of the most profound: "My times are in your hand." David's situation is desperate. In the previous verses in Psalm 31, he describes his extreme physical and emotional distress due to the attacks against him. He says, "My strength has failed ... my body has wasted away" (verse 10). "I am forgotten as a dead man.... I am like a broken vessel.... Terror is on every side" (verses 12-13).

David was in a horrible place, yet he yielded his agenda to God. He left the timing for when he would be delivered from his enemies up to God. David opened his hands, opened his heart, and gave his agenda over to God. He stretched out his hands to God and said, "Your timing, God, not mine."

Oh, that we would join David in saying, "But as for me, I trust in you, O LORD. I say, 'You are my God.' My times are in your hand. I bow my times of waiting. I worship you." Do you see? Do you understand? The Holy One receives these sweet words as worship. This worship is private, beautiful, and a fragrant offering to the Father.

COME, LET'S GET PRACTICAL

Does all of this sound a bit lofty, a bit difficult to apply? When you feel exhausted from waiting, how are you supposed to keep on waiting? How can we turn our times of waiting into times of worship? Let me give four practical suggestions, involving four strong verbs: *ask, stand, rock,* and *fly.* Yes, I know it sounds strange, but keep reading.

I. *Ask: Bring God your questions.* Bob Sorge, a pastor and worship leader, lost his voice due to a medical error during an operation. If anyone needs his voice, it is a pastor and worship leader. He writes,

> I have been very comforted by Psalm 27:4: "One thing I have desired of the LORD, that will I seek: That I may dwell in the house of the LORD all the days of my life, to behold the beauty of the LORD, and to inquire in His temple." I want to point to the invitation in the last phrase of that verse, "and to inquire in His temple." It is an invitation to come into His presence for the purpose of

questioning, asking, inquiring, searching out. Perhaps you've heard it said, "Don't question God," or "A Christian should never ask why," but that's not how I read this Scripture. I see this verse inviting us to bring our questions. Have you ever wondered, "God, what is happening to me? Lord, what are you doing in my life?" Bring those questions into His temple, and ask.[3]

I agree with Bob. Psalm 27 invites us to bring our questions into the presence of the Holy One and to inquire of Him. When I bring God my questions, I am usually on my knees and most likely weeping. I do not cry easily, but if I am in anguish, I am weeping when I come before my God. Our questions and tears do not scare the Lord. He is big enough to handle them, and He wants us to be real with Him.

One caution: When we bring our questions to God, we need to wait for His answer. We must not throw our questions at Him and then go to a friend and complain, "I can't understand what God is doing to me." Such actions constitute unbelief. So after you bring God your questions, hold your ground, even if you are still in the dark about why you are waiting or about how long you will wait.

2. *Stand: Hold your ground.* Earlier you met Valerie, my friend who has gone from running marathons to waiting in maternity clothes. I wish you could know this woman of faith. She called me recently and said, "This morning the Lord whispered to me, 'Valerie, your assignment is to wait. Are you up to the task?'" She went on to say that after spending the morning quietly before the Lord, she told Him, "Lord, I'm not up to the task at all, but you are, and you live in me so I say 'yes.'"

Valerie wrote me the following reflections on her years of waiting.

Can we speak of God's power only after we've been healed or after we survive the struggle we find ourselves in? Why are testimonies of how awesome God is typically announced after the fact? Is there not testimony of His saving grace in the midst of my crumbling? Can I only proclaim His goodness in the absence of disease? Doesn't He speak of who He IS in the agony of my brokenness? Is He less when I am less? NO. He is my ALL in ALL. I have to stand (even when I've lost my balance) on the solid rock of Jesus. He is my Sustainer and Redeemer in my weakness. He knows what it is like to be broken. He alone understands why I can't stand up. I know nothing, save His power. Maybe that is how I glorify Him: recognizing I need nothing else, not even my health.

So this is where I am today. It is not pretty. I have no mountaintop from which to report. This valley seems deep and very foggy. It can be a lonely place to hang out. But God is here. If He wasn't, I could not breathe. I trust He is steering, but I cannot see. He will get me through. I trust. I believe. I wait. That's all.

I thank God for the privilege of walking through the valley of waiting with this precious woman who encourages me.

Valerie has been prayed over and anointed with oil numerous times. She's fasted, read, and claimed Scriptures for multitudes of hours. She's written out Bible verses and memorized them. She's journaled, put on the armor of God, and claimed the blood of Christ. She has asked God that her pain not be wasted and prayed for others in their pain. She's gone on silent retreats. You name it, Valerie has done it. How does she survive? She told me,

Linda, I am hiding in His embrace, nestling close to Him. It is the only way I can survive. And I am standing. I have done everything I know to do . . . medically and spiritually. The apostle Paul says, when you have done all, STAND — so I'm STANDING — wobbly sometimes but standing because His arms hold me tight.

3. *Rock: Get in your chair.* One of my favorite verses is Micah 7:7: "But as for me, I will watch expectantly for the LORD; I will wait for the God of my salvation. My God will hear me."

While I want to do what this verse says, I find it confusing. How do I "watch expectantly" and "wait patiently" at the same time? Aren't they opposing actions? So I went to the Lord and asked Him how I could do both of these things. I recorded my prayer and His response in my journal:

> *God, you ask me to wait patiently and watch expectantly. Holy One, show me how these two concepts go together. They seem diametrically opposed. When I wait patiently, it's as if I'm sitting back in the chair, relaxed, serene . . . waiting for as long as it takes . . . waiting for your timeline. When I watch expectantly, it's as if I'm sitting on the edge of a chair, peering into the future with vibrant anticipation that you will answer at any moment.*
>
> *As I prayed, the Lord showed me the picture of a rocking chair. He asked me to go to my rocking chair and rock. So I did. I rocked back and thought, Ah, this is waiting patiently. Then I rocked forward and thought, This is watching expectantly. Yes, my Lord, I see. It is a continuous motion. Both can happen at once. Oh, my Beloved, teach me how to rock, waiting with patience and watching with expectancy. Take me by the hand*

and teach me. I want to live expecting you will answer any moment but bowing my agenda and waiting with patience for your timing. Help me Lord. Burn the image of the rocking chair into my heart.

For the last eight years I've been rocking forward and back, waiting for God to answer a prayer about someone I love. I choose to do what David did, to wait patiently, to wait on God alone. To bow to God's timeline. It is a much better place to be than where Sarah or Peter was. Is it always easy? You know the answer to that. But when I bow to God's timeline, it is worship! And I get to learn to fly!

4. *Fly: Be an eagle.* God has extended us an invitation to soar like an eagle! I love these beautiful verses that promise what my heart desires.

> Do you not know? Have you not heard?
>   The Everlasting God, the LORD, the Creator
> of the ends of the earth
>   Does not become weary or tired.
>   His understanding is inscrutable.
> He gives strength to the weary,
>   And to him who lacks might He increases
> power.
> Though youths grow weary and tired,
>   And vigorous young men stumble badly,
> Yet those who wait for the LORD
>   Will gain new strength;
>   They will mount up with wings like eagles,
>   They will run and not get tired,
>   They will walk and not become weary. (Isaiah
> 40:28-31)

These glorious verses follow a passage where God is revealed as the Everlasting and Almighty One. Andrew Murray expresses it well. "It is as that revelation enters into our soul that the waiting will become the spontaneous expression of what we know Him to be — a God altogether most worthy to be waited upon."[4] It is only as we truly see God as He is, Almighty and Everlasting and totally worthy of our trust, even when we don't understand His ways, that we can bow our times of waiting and worship Him.

Do you see the contrasts in these glorious verses? We grow weary, but God never does. We lack strength and might, but God is full of power. He desires to give His overflowing power to us. And when and how do we receive this abundance? When we wait on the Lord. Those who wait are given the precious promise that they will gain new strength. Not just ordinary, run-of-the-mill strength, but supernatural strength. God has given those who wait on Him a magnificent promise: They will mount up with wings like eagles, run and not grow weary. This is what we need. But as appealing as it sounds, the path to flight is not easy. To understand this, we only have to reflect on how eagles are taught the use of their wings. In your mind's eye, envision two young eaglets and their mother in a nest on a towering cliff rising a thousand feet out of the sea. Observe the mother bird stir up her nest with her beak and then push the timid birds out of the warm nest and over the precipice. How cruel her action appears as the eaglets plunge down, down, down . . . but then watch how the mother bird tenderly swoops under her baby eaglets, capturing them at the last moment on her wings before they crash on the rocks. She carries them to safety and lovingly places them in the shelter of their warm nest. Then once again look as the mother eagle stirs up the nest. Oh, how the babies loudly squawk in protest as they are cast over the ledge. But in time, they stretch out their untrained wings and begin to fly.

Your Father God also wants to teach you how to fly. So, He stirs up your nest. He disappoints your hopes. He allows you to be discouraged. He makes you wait and wait and wait. You feel weary and helpless and without strength. Look up! Do you see Him coming? He spreads His strong wings out for you to rest upon. He asks you to sink down into Him and wait on Him, and He promises to gently carry you until your strength is renewed and you can fly.

My friend, the Lord Jesus sees your pain. He prays for you with deep affection. Will you pause and name the person or thing God desires for you to bow to His timeline? He knows you are waiting. He loves you. He tenderly asks, "Will you trust me and worship me by saying, 'My times are in your hand'?"

Waiting

Desperately, helplessly, longingly, I cried.
Quietly, patiently, lovingly God replied.
I pled and I wept for a clue to my fate,
And the Master so gently said, "Child, you must wait!"

"Wait? You say, wait!" my indignant reply.
"Lord, I need answers, I need to know why!
Is your hand shortened? Or have you not heard?
By FAITH I have asked, and am claiming your Word.

"My future and all to which I can relate
Hangs in the balance, and you tell me to WAIT?
I'm needing a yes, a go-ahead sign,
Or even a 'no' to which I can resign.

"And Lord, you promised that if we believe
We need but to ask, and we shall receive.
And Lord, I've been asking, and this is my cry:
I'm weary of asking! I need a reply!"

Then quietly, softly, I learned of my fate
As my Master replied once again, "You must wait."
So, I slumped in my chair, defeated and taut
And grumbled to God, "So, I'm waiting . . . for what?"

He seemed then to kneel and His eyes wept with mine.
And he tenderly said, "I could give you a sign.
I could shake the heavens, and darken the sun.
I could raise the dead, and cause mountains to run.

"All you seek, I could give, and pleased you would be.
You would have what you want — but, you wouldn't know ME.

You'd not know the depth of my love for each saint;
You'd not know the power that I give to the faint;

"You'd not learn to see through the clouds of despair;
You'd not learn to trust just by knowing I'm there;
You'd not know the joy of resting in me
When darkness and silence were all you could see.

"You'd never experience that fullness of love
As the peace of my Spirit descends like a dove;
You'd know that I give and I save ... (for a start),
But you'd not know the depth of the beat of my heart.

"The glow of my comfort late into the night,
The faith that I give when you walk without sight,
The depth that's beyond getting just what you asked
Of an infinite God, who makes what you have LAST.

"You'd never know, should your pain quickly flee,
What it means that 'My grace is sufficient for thee.'
Yes, your dreams for your loved ones overnight would come true,
But, oh, the loss! if I lost what I'm doing in you!

"So, be silent, my child, and in time you will see
THAT THE GREATEST OF GIFTS IS TO GET TO KNOW ME.
And though oft may my answers seem terribly late,
My wisest of answers is still but to WAIT."[5]

Chapter 10

I
Bow
My
Pain

Chapter 10

I Bow My Pain

Come let us worship and bow down,

Let us bow our pain and worship God.

Psalm 95:6, AUTHOR'S PARAPHRASE

It appeared to be a typical baptism. Jesus, dressed in a casual linen tunic and sandals, walked into the Jordan River to be baptized by his cousin, John. But there was nothing normal about this glorious, supernatural event. The heavens majestically parted. Looking very much like a white dove, the Holy Spirit descended and alighted upon Jesus. Next, the booming voice of God the Father thundered through the heavens, and the words, oh, the words! Could more beautiful words be heard in all the earth? "You are My beloved Son, in You I am well-pleased" (Mark 1:11).

The next word in the gospel is the word *immediately*. Something happened right after the Father spoke these special words of affirmation to His Son. Was the beloved Son invited to a celebration banquet? No. Did the One who so pleased the Father receive an all-expenses paid vacation? No. Did the crowd of onlookers lift Jesus on their shoulders and parade Him back into town? No. What happened was this:

> *Immediately* the Holy Spirit compelled Jesus to go into the wilderness to be tempted by Satan. (Mark 1:12, AUTHOR'S PARAPHRASE)

If this doesn't make sense to you, join the club. It makes no sense to me either. The same Holy Spirit who descends from God's

183

throne and alights on Jesus with a special anointing immediately compels Him to venture out into the wilderness and into deep pain. The same Voice that one moment dramatically declares His love and pleasure in His Son, the next moment sentences that Son to forty days of pain — no food, no water, and fierce temptation from the enemy. So much for thinking that when you please God, He blesses you with a pain-free life in return. Certainly the last thing on your mind is that God's response when you delight Him is to lead you into a place of deep pain. Yet this is exactly what happened to Jesus.

We see the same scenario in one of my favorite books, *Hinds' Feet on High Places*. Much Afraid, the main character in this beautiful allegory, is on a journey with the Good Shepherd to the High Places, which symbolizes God's presence. The Shepherd tells her that He is sending two companions to encourage her on her journey. She expects them to be Joy and Peace. But to her shock and dismay, her travel mates are Sorrow and Suffering. Sorrow and Suffering lead Much Afraid to a desert. Much Afraid calls to the Shepherd.

> "Shepherd," she said despairingly, "I can't understand this. The guides you gave me say that we must go down there into that desert, turning right away from the High Places altogether. You don't mean that, do you? You can't contradict yourself. Tell them we are not to go there, and show us another way. Make a way for us, Shepherd, as you promised."
>
> He looked at her and answered very gently, "That is the path, Much Afraid, and you are to go down there."[1]

The way to God's presence often involves sorrow and suffering and time in a desert. I don't know about you, but I don't like the sound of "desert time." I much prefer Jesus' words, "I came that they may have life, and have it abundantly" (John 10:10). In my naiveté as a young believer, I thought *abundant* meant no detours, no desert time, and no pain.

While a life without pain sounds good, it's just not biblical. The same Lord Jesus who talks about an abundant life also says, "In the world you have tribulation, but take courage; I have over-come the world" (John 16:33). A major theme in the Bible is how to live in the midst of trials, pressures, and pain. There is a place that is pressure-free, a glorious land where all tears will be wiped away, where death, mourning, crying, and pain are no more, but it is called heaven, not earth (see Revelation 21:4). Until we arrive in eternity, we live in a world of sickness, strife, sadness, and sin, where every part of us groans for heaven, and like little Much Afraid, our minds fill with unanswered questions:

If God is so powerful, why doesn't He prevent pain and suffering?

How can a loving God allow pain, sickness, and suffering?

And often our questions are personal.

Why did God let my baby die?

Where was God when my husband first looked at porn?

Why didn't God save me from sexual abuse?

These important questions require much prayer and thought. If you are asking these types of questions, read some of the books listed on page 202, as they will be helpful to you. Since this is a book about worship as a lifestyle, the question we are considering in this chapter is:

How do I bow my pain before God as an act of worship?

You're thinking, *Bow my pain? Are you serious, Linda? Why don't you tell me how to get rid of pain?*

We all would like to eliminate pain because we know it's a bitter taste. Whether its source is physical, emotional, mental, or spiritual, pain intercepts our hopes and plans and rearranges our dreams. One woman describes her pain like this: "It truly feels like everything is falling down around me, and everything is falling apart within me."

If you are like me, when you think of biblical characters who have suffered, your mind immediately goes to Job, Joseph, and David, the writer of psalms of lament. But what picture fills your mind when you think of the apostle Paul? A strong, articulate apostle who wrote many books of the New Testament? All true, but it is also true that Paul experienced great physical pain. In 2 Corinthians we are given a glimpse into his life and the hardships he suffered. We meet Paul, the man — not Paul, the apostle, or Paul, the intellectual genius and orator — just Paul, the man who suffered. Listen to his piercing words from 2 Corinthians.

> I have worked harder, been put in prison more often, been whipped times without number, and faced death again and again. Five different times the Jewish leaders gave me thirty-nine lashes. Three times I was beaten with rods. Once I was stoned. Three times I was shipwrecked. Once I spent a whole night and a day adrift at sea. I have traveled on many long journeys. I have faced danger from rivers and from robbers. I have faced danger from my own people, the Jews, as well as from the Gentiles. I have faced danger in the cities, in the deserts, and on the seas. And I have faced dangers from men who claim to be believers but are not. I have worked hard and long, enduring many sleepless nights. I have been hungry and thirsty and have often gone without food. I have shivered in the cold, without enough clothing to keep me warm. (11:23-27, NLT)

The apostle Paul was an expert in physical pain, but he also knew emotional pain. He said that everyone in Asia had deserted him (see 2 Timothy 1:15). Any of us who have been rejected by one friend knows this pain is agonizing. But to be deserted by an entire continent? I can't even imagine. As an old man facing martyrdom, Paul felt lonely and isolated. He begged his friends to come quickly in order to be with him in his final days on earth (see 2 Timothy 4:21).

Paul walked through deserts of pain with his soul lifted to God in worship. My soul has personally been revived, encouraged, and motivated by the things he wrote in 2 Corinthians. I love Paul's perspective. He suffered many varieties of pain, yet his mantra was, "I do not give up; I do not give up." Because Paul made the choice to not give up, he was strengthened in beautiful ways. He:

- Experienced God's comfort.
- Exchanged self-confidence for God-confidence.
- Chose to live on the side of triumph.
- Allowed his pain to become a fragrant offering.

Paul begins his words to the church at Corinth by telling them that God will comfort them in their pain. We see two parts to God's comfort. First, He comforts us, then we are able to comfort others.

PAUL EXPERIENCED GOD'S COMFORT

> All praise to God, the Father of our Lord Jesus Christ. God is our merciful Father and the source of all comfort. He comforts us in all our troubles so that we can comfort others. When they are troubled, we will be able to give them the same comfort God has given us. (2 Corinthians 1:3-4, NLT)

Do you know the soft comfort of God? He is called the God of All Comfort. It is a glorious name, and the arms of His comfort are more tender than any earthly arms. I see His comfort as a billowy cloud. When troubles engulf me, I fall back into the soft cloud of His tender care. During seasons of pain, I have experienced the deep comfort of my Father. I know well the comfort of the Encourager, the Holy Spirit in my life.

What does this comfort look like? Let me take you into my life three years ago. I had been planning for six months. My four children, their mates, and all my grandchildren were coming for Christmas. My children live on the East Coast and West Coast, and I live in Colorado, so I was thrilled to have everyone under one roof. I was sure our time together would be glorious. I was wrong. Instead of building beautiful memories, we experienced division, discord, and dissent. Never in my wildest imaginings could I have envisioned this. I cried for twenty-four hours straight.

How did God comfort me during my time of disappointment? On Monday while reading God's Word, the Holy Spirit illumined Romans 5:3-5 — it was as if the verses were written just for me.

> And not only this, but we also exult in our tribulations, knowing that tribulation brings about perseverance; and perseverance, proven character; and proven character, hope; and hope does not disappoint, because the love of God has been poured out within our hearts through the Holy Spirit who was given to us.

Yes, Lord, I can give thanks for this pain because you promise that this trial will build perseverance, character, and hope in me! Your hope will not disappoint me . . . thank you, Lord. I'd forgotten these wonderful verses. I tucked God's promises in my mind and heart, and His words sustained me.

On Tuesday a friend from another state emailed me: *Linda, as I prayed for you today, God reminded me that He sings over you with joy! He loves you so much, dear Linda. Whatever you are going through right now, He cares!*

On Wednesday I poured out my grief before God. The Holy Spirit wept through me with deep, wrenching sobs. In a precious and personal way, I sensed His heart for my pain. I felt as if God had hugged me. On Thursday, a woman came to me in deep pain over her family. As I prayed over her, God used me to comfort her with the comfort He had given me! How I rejoiced!

Paul learned to comfort others by first receiving God's comfort. When we have experienced His comfort, like Paul, we can then give comfort to others. I like how Alan Redpath describes this ministry of comfort. "But if any of us know the Lord Jesus Christ in reality then God opens for each of His children a ministry which is unique — a ministry of comfort, which simply means the ability to communicate Holy Spirit life to others."[2] This godly man, whose ministry of preaching and writing touched lives all over the globe, went on to say, "Personally, I would rather have the spiritual gift of bringing life to one broken heart than the ability to preach a thousand sermons."[3] According to God, you and I can participate in this ministry of bringing life to another in need.

Paul learned about comfort through his pain. Next, he learned to rely *only* on God.

Paul Exchanged Self-Confidence for God-Confidence

We were crushed and overwhelmed beyond our ability to endure, and we thought we would never live through it. In fact, we expected to die. But as a result, we stopped relying on ourselves and learned to rely only on God, who raises the dead.
(2 Corinthians 1:8-9, NLT)

Right now you may be experiencing a crushed and over-whelmed time in your life. If so, know that this painful crush-ing has a high purpose. I know without a shadow of a doubt that God's purpose for Linda Dillow has been to crush any faith I have in my abilities, talents, cleverness, and controlling strategies. He has used pressure and pain to bring me to the end of my self-confidence. God has one great purpose for all of us above every-thing else: "It is to destroy in us forever any possible confidence in the flesh; it is to bring us to the place where self-confidence has passed into history and has been exchanged for a confidence in God, who raises the dead."[4]

God-confidence is a song of faith in the night and the highest form of worship. It shows that you believe God's Word to you to be true, and that you trust Him to fulfill it.

As I look back on the painful times in my life, I rejoice that because of them:

- I've learned to trust God in the dark for what I don't understand, for what doesn't make sense to me.
- I've been deepened as a person, given empathy for others in pain.
- I've received comfort from God, and thus been able to comfort others with the Holy Spirit's comfort I've received.

We have seen that a higher purpose in pain is to impart com-fort and God-confidence in us. Look with me now at one of Paul's amazing, hope-filled statements. It will fill you with courage.

PAUL LEARNED TO LIVE ON THE SIDE OF TRIUMPH

We are hard pressed on every side, but not crushed; perplexed, but not in despair; persecuted, but not abandoned; struck down, but not destroyed. (2 Corinthians 4:8-9, NIV)

Look carefully at these verses. Do you see the "but nots"? There are four of them. Four words of agony on the left side of "but not," and four words of triumph on the right side. Our challenge is to learn to live on the side of triumph.

The Side of Agony	The Side of Triumph
1. Hard Pressed	BUT NOT Crushed
2. Perplexed	BUT NOT in Despair
3. Persecuted	BUT NOT Abandoned
4. Struck Down	BUT NOT Destroyed

Let's look at each of these four phrases, and I will introduce you to some special women who have learned to live on the side of triumph.

1. Paul Was Hard Pressed, BUT NOT Crushed. (2 Corinthians 4:8)

The Greek word translated here as "hard pressed" suggests the idea of being hemmed in a narrow space from which there is no exit.[5] Most of us have felt this suffocating pressure that makes us feel as if we will cave in. It is not a pleasant place to be.

Janae experienced this hard-pressed feeling when a shocking revelation shattered her world. During a supposedly romantic weekend with her husband, she learned that throughout their marriage, he had been involved in sexual sin. I'll let Janae tell you how she responded.

> Anguish . . . terror . . . fear . . . trembling . . . revulsion. Psalm 55 where David said, "If an enemy were insulting me, I could endure it; if a foe were raising himself against me, I could hide from him. But it is you . . . my companion, my close friend, with whom I once enjoyed sweet fellowship as we walked with the throng at the house of God." David's words describe my heart's cry as I desperately tried to process my husband's betrayal.
>
> I turned to God's Word, as it seemed to give me my next breath on some days. When my mind wanted to go to the dark places of my husband's sin, God used His Word to capture my heart and mind. I drank in the Psalms. I memorized the Psalms and God used the Scripture, worship music, and praise journaling to begin to heal my broken heart.
>
> It has been a long, arduous journey to bow my pain before a sovereign God and to let Him write a new story for my marriage.

All of us, like Paul and Janae, will face times when we feel pressed in, with no way of escape. But be encouraged! You don't have to be crushed!

2. Paul Was Perplexed, BUT NOT in Despair. (2 Corinthians 4:8)

Pain is confusing, and often God's response to illness, grief, and deep anguish is perplexing. I often don't understand His ways. Neither did the apostle Paul. But God's Word encourages us: We do not have to be in despair. Why? Because we know that God can either make us strong in our weakness so that we can persevere, or He can deliver us from our pain at any moment. In Valerie's case, He did both.

In the last chapter, I told you about Valerie and how her doctors at Mayo Clinic and Stanford Medical Center were unable to tell her what was causing her abdomen to be engorged. No one had answers to her questions. She continued to wear maternity clothes. Despite her perplexity and pain, she stood strong in her faith. Even after five years of living with this pain, she did not despair. Like Paul, Valerie chose to trust and worship in her pain.

Then on Day 621 of wearing maternity clothes, as Valerie returned from taking her children to school, she felt something happening in her stomach. For ten minutes she watched her bulging abdomen shrink. The swelling was gone! Valerie was healed! On a CD are three ultrasounds, one taken the day before her healing and two taken in the week following. These scientific results loudly declare that she is healed. The doctors ask, "How is this possible?" and Valerie replies, "GOD!" Oh, how I worshipped Him with shouts of praise and tears of joy when I heard the news. I cannot contain my gratitude for this miraculous healing.

Will God always provide a way of escape from your perplexing prison of pain if you bow and worship Him? Yes, but His way of escape may not be instantaneous deliverance. Sometimes His way of escape is to fling open the doors of disease, oppression, and heartache, and in an instant, heal; other times His way of escape is to give us the peace and grace to endure our pain.

God chose to supernaturally heal Valerie. He chose not to heal Paul of his "thorn in the flesh" (2 Corinthians 12:7). Paul begged God three times to take away his painful "thorn," and God's response was, "'My grace is all you need. My power works best in weakness.' So now I am glad to boast about my weaknesses, so that the power of Christ can work through me. That's why I take pleasure in my weaknesses, and in the insults, hardships, persecutions, and troubles that I suffer for Christ. For when I am weak, then I am strong" (2 Corinthians 12:9-10, NLT).

I see two extremes in the Christian community concerning God's healing power. Some claim healing for everyone. A man recently learned I was still suffering from migraine headaches, and he immediately laid hands on me, asked God for healing, and declared the headaches gone (which they weren't). On the other side, some Christians give lip service to the fact that God is the Healer, but they act and live as if God does not heal bodies, relationships, or anything. I am convinced that God heals today, and I have been privileged to see His supernatural healing power in the life of Valerie. But often He allows our perplexing pain to continue, while providing us with the strength to endure.

3. Paul Was Persecuted, BUT NOT Abandoned. (2 Corinthians 4:9)

Oswald Chambers says, "God does not keep a man immune from trouble; He says, 'I will be with him in trouble.' I am sorry for the Christian who has not something in his circumstances he wishes was not there."[6] Trials may come upon you, people may come against you, but God has promised, He will never abandon you. "'I will never desert you, nor will I ever forsake you, so that we confidently say, 'The Lord is my Helper, I will not be afraid. What will man do to me?'" (Hebrews 13:5-6).

Erin needed to know that God would never desert or forsake her, as her earthly father had done. This man, who should have loved and protected her, had horribly abused her sexually. Not only did he abuse and torture her, but he gave her to others in a satanic cult to be sacrificed sexually to evil. Her persecution and pain are indescribable, but as you will see from her journal entry below, she was not abandoned.

> Lord, I am so tired of this horrific road I am
> walking on . . . but how blessed I am that you walk

beside me . . . at times carrying me . . . at times
shielding me . . . at times holding me back . . . at
times encouraging me forward . . . always, always,
always comforting me with your love. I would
walk this road forever, Lord, if it means more of
you. Whatever it takes to know you intimately,
Lord, is what I want . . . no matter the cost . . . no
matter how terrifyingly difficult the way is . . . I
will go if it means more of you. You are everything
to me. . . . I don't care how great the pain . . . the
grief . . . the suffering . . . the anguish . . . if it
brings me to your holy throne . . . if it brings you
great glory . . . I will go. I love you more than life
itself. The depth of this pain only magnifies the
depth of my love for you.

Erin wrote the following song:

I Bow My Pain

Lord, I want to worship you
with all my pain
with all my tears
that fall like rain
Lord, I want to honor you
with all my grief
with all my heartache
as I weep
Lord, I want to serve you
in all that I do
Please take my aching heart, Lord,
and focus it on you

Chorus:
All that I want
is your beautiful face
before my eyes
Your holiness
that reaches out to me
All that I need
is your tender embrace
around my heart
your gentleness
that covers all of me

Lord, I want to worship you
as I am
All my hurt
I give to the Lamb
Lord, I want to honor you
with all my suffering
Even in this darkness
you are my King
Lord, I bow before you
and cry at your feet
Please take these humble offerings
and fill me with your peace

4. Paul Was Struck Down, BUT NOT Destroyed. (2 Corinthians 4:9)

What does it mean to be "struck down, but not destroyed"? In the Greek, the word picture is of a fighter who has been hit and struck down by his opponent and is awaiting his death blow. Then, against all odds, he rises to his feet once again. He is not destroyed because he has not been abandoned. God Almighty is beside him and lifts him up when he falls.[7]

Sarah, a pastor's wife, felt struck down by the pervasive pain of her violent, abusive family. She chose not to let the punches of life defeat her, but instead asked, "God, how can I bow this pain in worship?" Not long afterward, she wrote the following in an email to me:

> Linda, guess what Abba revealed to me this morning in my time of worship? Remember how I told you that the pain and disappointments in my life had dug a huge chasm between God and me? The chasm makes Him seem invisible and far away. Now I see that worship — truly bowing my heart and soul, even when I am afraid, anxious, angry, and upset — is the ONLY thing that can bridge that gap and mysteriously draw me into His presence. Grieving helped me get to the point where I could truly fall down on my face and give Him my heart, but it wasn't enough. I had to go one step further, giving up the control that had become an idol for me. I had to bow my pain and worship His holy name.

Dear woman who desires to bow your pain, you have a choice: You can live on the side of agony: hard pressed, perplexed, persecuted, and struck down — OR you can live on the side of triumph: BUT NOT crushed, BUT NOT in despair, BUT NOT abandoned, BUT NOT destroyed. Like Janae, Valerie, Erin, Sarah, and scores of other women, you can live on the side of triumph. As you bow your pain in worship, it can become a fragrant offering to your God.

PAUL'S PAIN BECOMES A FRAGRANT OFFERING

> But thank God! He has made us his captives and continues to lead us along in Christ's triumphal procession. Now He uses us to spread the knowledge of Christ everywhere, like sweet perfume. Our lives are a Christ-like fragrance rising up to God. (2 Corinthians 2:14-15, NLT)

Is a sweet-smelling perfume rising from your life? The following thought-provoking story has caused me to think about the fragrance of my life.

A young woman told her mother that the pain in her life was so difficult that she wanted to give up. She was tired of fighting and struggling. As soon as one problem was solved, a new one arose. The mother took the girl to the kitchen and filled three pots with water. In the first she placed carrots, in the second she placed eggs, and in the last she placed ground coffee beans. She let them sit and boil, without saying a word.

In about twenty minutes the woman turned off the burners. She fished the carrots out and placed them in a bowl. She pulled the eggs out and placed them in the bowl. Then she ladled the coffee out and placed it in a cup. Turning to her daughter, she asked, "Tell me, what do you see?" "Carrots, eggs, and coffee," came the reply. The mother then brought her daughter closer and asked her to feel the carrots. She did and noted that they were soft. The mother then asked the girl to take an egg and break it. After pulling off the shell, she observed the hard-boiled egg. Finally, the mother asked the daughter to sip the coffee. She smiled as she tasted its rich flavor, and then asked, "What's the point, Mom?"

Her mother explained that each of these objects had faced the same adversity — boiling water — but each reacted differently.

The carrot went in strong and hard, but after being subjected to the boiling water, it softened and became weak. The egg had been fragile. Its thin, outer shell had protected its liquid inside, its inside had become hardened. The ground coffee beans were unique, however. After they were in the boiling water, they had changed the water.

"Which are you?" the mother asked her daughter. "When adversity knocks on your door, how do you respond? Are you a carrot, an egg, or a coffee bean?"[8]

I have thought long and hard about this question, and I have asked myself, "Am I the carrot that seems strong, but wilts and becomes soft when faced with pain and adversity? Am I the egg that starts with a malleable heart, but becomes hardened with the heat? Or, am I like the coffee bean that releases a pleasing flavor and fragrance in the very circumstances that bring my pain?" How would you describe yourself? Are you a carrot, an egg, or a coffee bean?

C. H. Spurgeon wrote that our grief cannot mar the melody of our praise, it is simply the bass notes of our life song, "To God Be the Glory."

My friend, will you bow your pain? Will you ask God to make you like the coffee bean? To help you do this, consider implementing these practical suggestions.

Come, Let's Get Practical

1. *When you find yourself in the midst of pain, sing songs of praise to God.* As you worship the Lord, the atmosphere changes. When Paul and Silas were in jail, they began to sing and worship their God. And what happened? Their spirit of worship became a weapon against the enemy and the doors of their prison were opened wide.

In Isaiah 61:3 we read that a spirit of despair is to be replaced with a garment of praise. "No exercise or medicine will cure the ill of discouragement like praise. Depression and praise cannot long live in the same heart. They are absolutely incompatible room-mates. Praise brings the consciousness of the presence of God and the liars from the pit cannot effectively market their wares in an atmosphere of praise. Since it is a garment, we can make a choice to put it on as we do a shirt, a blouse, or a coat."[9] The constant wearing of a garment of praise will ward off what comes during a season of pain: discouragement, despair, and depression.

How do you praise? I have special CDs that are just for times of pain. I put on the songs of hope, fall to my knees, and worship Him for who He is: my Deliverer, my Refuge, my Strong Tower, my Hiding Place, and so much more. As I worship Him for who He is, the garment of praise replaces discouragement and my soul is filled with hope in the midst of my pain.

2. *When you are in pain, claim Scripture.* When you feel crushed, claim Psalm 9:9: "The LORD also will be a stronghold for the oppressed, a stronghold in times of trouble."

When you are confused, without light for your way, claim Psalm 18:28-29: "For You light my lamp; the LORD my God illumines my darkness. For by You I can run upon a troop; and by my God I can leap over a wall."

When you feel abandoned, claim Psalm 9:10: "And those who know Your name will put their trust in You, for You, O LORD, have not forsaken those who seek You."

When you feel struck down, claim Psalm 31:24. "Be strong and let your heart take courage, all you who hope in the LORD."

3. *When you are in pain, weep before God.* There is no relief so great as the relief experienced through the outpouring of tears. My first lessons in private worship were in weeping before God. When I had no words, my companion, the Holy Spirit, lifted my wrenching sobs to my Father. We are told in Scripture that this is one of the Spirit's jobs. "The Spirit also helps our weakness; for we do not

know how to pray as we should, but the Spirit Himself intercedes for us with groanings too deep for words" (Romans 8:26).

Go before the God of all comfort, and ask Him to envelop you with the sweetness of His comforting embrace.

4. *When you are in pain — persevere — don't give up!* My friend, this week find a time to get away alone for half an hour and write a prayer to God, telling Him why you choose to persevere. As you write, consider all of Paul's encouraging statements from 2 Corinthians. Two times Paul says, "We do not give up, we do not give up!" (see 4:1,16).

As you are with the Lord, think about traditional Chinese puppet theater, which is acted out on two levels at the same time. The lower level shows the characters as they progress moment-by-moment through the trials and conflicts of the story. On the upper level, however, the audience can see how the play concludes, as the villains are punished and the heroes are rewarded. Because the audience can already see the outcome by looking up, they're not worried when the situation looks grave and the bad guys start to gain the upper hand. Instead, they get vocally involved. They begin shouting encouragement at the harried characters on the lower lever. "Don't quit! Don't stop! Don't give up! We know you're going to make it!"[10]

As you write out your prayer this week, remember that God the Father and God the Son are shouting encouragement to you from heaven. God the Spirit is shouting encouragement from within. All the angelic host join the Three in One, "Don't quit! Don't stop! Don't give up! Keep worshipping through your pain."

Suggested Reading List About Pain

A Sacred Sorrow by Michael Card
A Deeper Kind of Calm by Linda Dillow
A Grace Disguised by Jerry Sittser
Disappointment with God by Philip Yancey
The Fire of Delayed Answers by Bob Sorge
When God Doesn't Make Sense by Dr. James Dobson
When God Is Silent by Ron Dunn
When God Weeps by Joni Eareckson Tada

I

Bow

My

Will

Chapter 11

I Bow My Will

I take joy in doing your will, my God,
for your instructions are written on my heart.

PSALM 40:8, NLT

I am waiting for the book *The Strong-Willed Dog* to be written. Our white Samoyed, Tasha, could have written such a book. Always, Tasha wanted to do what Tasha wanted to do. When this lovely snow-white creature would escape the confines of the fence, I would run after her shouting, "Tasha, come here!" Stopping long enough to turn, cock her head, and look me in the eye, she would then continue on her merry way, not "coming here" but "going there."

Some of you have battled wills with dogs, others of you with children.

I remember . . . being the mother of three little ones, three and under. I was a very tired mommy, and Tommy, the youngest of my three, had asthma. I have many memories of those years, rushing to the hospital in the middle of the night with vomit all over me and the car from Tommy's choking cough. I remember sleeping on a mat by his crib and trying to feed my darling son. He was under a croup tent, and I had to reach through the slats in his crib. This was a very messy, unpopular affair for both Tommy and Mommy. But my most vivid memory is of the 3 a.m. shower detail. Doctor's orders were that when my son could not breathe, I was to turn the hot shower on full strength and close the door. When the bathroom was filled with steam, I was to take Tommy and sit on the potty (lid down, of course) and wait for the steam to work its

205

wonders on his bronchial tubes and lungs. Believe me, this was not a fun "Mom and son time."

Tommy wasn't the only one with an intense dislike of the steam cave. This mommy found little joy in her middle-of-the-night wrestling matches with a squirming, screeching toddler. Before he could talk, Tommy would fight me, pound my chest, and wail like a wounded coyote. After he could talk, he would pound and shout, "Out, Mommy, out!"

How pleased I would have been if Tommy had said, "Oh, Mommy, I know you love me and want only my best. I don't understand why I have to be in this hot, steamy place, but I'll sit quietly while the steam does its work."

I remember . . . being the mother of four teenagers. One of these very wonderful teens had been born with a will of iron. This teen was completely disgusted with our "conservative rules" and believed that every kid on the planet had more privileges than we permitted. Each week that teen argued with Jody and me about which movies were permitted, which parties were acceptable. The atmosphere of our home resembled a war zone. Guess who was labeled the enemy?

How pleased I would have been if our child had come to me and said, "Mom, your way doesn't make sense to me, but I know you love me and want what is best for me. I'll do what you think is right even though I don't understand."

I was wiser. I had lived more years. I saw all the pieces of the puzzle of my children's lives. I saw all the reasons behind the rules *and* I loved my kids! They should have known my deep love for them and trusted me — even when they didn't understand.

Why am I telling you this? Because I see an analogy between how my children related to me and how I relate to my heavenly Father. There was a time I was a *toddler* before God. I would pound on His chest and scream, "Let me out of this steamy bathroom! I don't like what's happening!" There was also a time I was a *teenager* before God and would forcefully protest, "I planned my life, and

I've worked really hard. God, it's only fair that it work out the way I planned it. Please give me what I want NOW!"

I am grateful that I have moved beyond the toddler and teenage years. God is changing me into a *trusting one*. What is the difference between a teenager and a trusting one?

Teenager	Trusting One
Self-centered	God-centered
Independent	Dependent
Resistant	Submissive

A "Trusting One" humbly bows her will to God's will. Bowing my will is so hard to do, yet I am convinced this is the deepest form of worship. When I bow my will in worship, I put feet to my faith. I come to God with a spirit that says,

> *You, Holy God, see all the pieces of the puzzle of my life. And you love me. I trust you. I bow my will to you. You are better than I am. You are bigger than I am. You are wiser than I am. You are more than I am. I bow before your plan and purpose.*

The Lord Jesus exemplified this deep worship in the Garden of Gethsemane. Three times He went away alone and fell before the Father in agony and prayed, "My Father! If it is possible, let this cup of suffering be taken away from me. Yet I want your will to be done, not mine" (Matthew 26:39, NLT). In essence Jesus was saying, "My Father, I've put my request before you. Now I bow my will to yours."

Christ's purpose was "To do Your will, O God" (Hebrews 10:7). And God's will for His son was that He sacrifice Himself for us — that He suffer so that we might be healed. This was Jesus' act of worship. Bowing His will to the Father's will was agony for the Son of God. It is also agony for us.

God painted pictures in His Word of men and women who bowed their will to His. These portraits are for our instruction and encouragement. Look with me and learn from three men who lived out this deep worship: Job, Habakkuk, and Abraham.

JOB BOWED LOW

When you think of Job, do you visualize a man who struggled with God? Who challenged God? Yes, Job struggled and asked questions, but did you know that the day he lost all his possessions and his ten children, he *immediately* bowed his will in worship? His words in Job 1:20-21 astound me:

> Then Job arose and tore his robe and shaved his head, and he fell to the ground and worshiped. He said, "Naked I came from my mother's womb, and naked I shall return there. The LORD gave and the LORD has taken away. Blessed be the name of the LORD."

In humility, Job fell prostrate before the God who made no sense, before the God who had just taken away ALL his children. Job's breathtakingly beautiful words were his worship. Job bowed his will to God's will, and in essence said to the Almighty, "It is your right and privilege to give to me and your right and privilege to take away the gifts. Whatever happens I will bless your name!"

I have meditated often on Job's act of worship. It is almost inconceivable that *after* being told what he had been told, Job *immediately* fell on his face and said, "Blessed be the name of the LORD." His actions make me think of these words penned by Charles Spurgeon: "They are cheap songs which we give to God when we are rich. It is easy enough to kiss the hand of a giving God, but to bless Him when He takes away is to bless Him indeed."[1]

The beautiful worship song *Blessed Be Your Name* is based on Job's lament in Job 1:21. I cannot sing this song without seeing this man bent low with grief, yet bowed even lower in worship. On his face before God, he declared, "Blessed be your name when the road is marked with suffering, when there's pain in the offering, blessed be your name." Is there any deeper worship than this? I think not.

I have asked God to give me a heart of worship like Job's.

Job expressed his worship by bowing low before God. The Prophet Habakkuk's worship was a joyful dance.

Habakkuk Danced

If you have read my book *Calm My Anxious Heart,* you know that Habakkuk is one of my favorite books in the Bible. Why? Because this prophet always brings his problems and doubts to God instead of to people. Habakkuk had come before God with grief because of the sin of his country, Judah, begging God to intervene. God answers by declaring that yes, He will intervene. How? By sending the Babylonians to invade Judah and take the Jewish people captive. God's answer throws Habakkuk into total confusion. How could God do this?

As the book of Habakkuk progresses, this dear prophet moves from challenging God to worshipping Him. Congregations often quote one of Habakkuk's statements about the holy hush of worship: "But the LORD is in His holy temple. Let all the earth be silent before Him" (Habakkuk 2:20). The book ends with the prophet's statement of faith. He declares that even if everything is stripped away from him, all his security, everything that gives him sustenance . . .

> Yet I will exult in the LORD, I will *rejoice* in the God of my salvation. (Habakkuk 3:18, italics mine)

The word *rejoice* is very descriptive in the Hebrew language. It literally means to "spin around for joy."[2] Habakkuk declared that when the invasion by the Babylonians came, he would be dancing. Like Joni in her wheelchair, he would spin around with joy. He had bowed his will to God's will, even when he didn't understand, and he vowed to demonstrate his trust with exuberant worship.

Some people, when they don't understand God, might say in a resigned way, "Okay, God, I'll trust you." But how many will spin around for joy in their God when He makes no sense? Habakkuk was secure in God. He knew that the will of God would never take him where the grace of God would not protect him.

I have asked God to give me a heart of worship like Habakkuk's.

Habakkuk showed his deep faith by dancing joyously; Abraham showed his by building an altar.

ABRAHAM BUILT AN "ISAAC ALTAR"

I'm going to ask you to do something for me. When you read about Abraham offering Isaac in the upcoming passage, please do not tune out and think, *I already know what happens.* I believe God wants to teach you something new and beautiful through this story, where worship is mentioned for the first time in God's Word. So open your eyes, open your heart, and read it as if you've never heard the story before.

> God said, "Abraham!"
> "Yes?" answered Abraham. "I'm listening."
> He said, "Take your dear son Isaac whom you love and go to the land of Moriah. Sacrifice him there as a burnt offering on one of the mountains that I'll point out to you."
> Abraham got up early in the morning and

saddled his donkey. He took two of his young servants and his son Isaac. He had split wood for the
burnt offering. He set out for the place God had
directed him. On the third day he looked up and
saw the place in the distance. Abraham told his
two young servants, "Stay here with the donkey.
The boy and I are going over there to worship;
then we'll come back to you."

Abraham took the wood for the burnt offering and gave it to Isaac his son to carry. He carried the flint and the knife. The two of them went
off together.

Isaac said to Abraham his father, "Father?"

"Yes, my son."

"We have flint and wood, but where's the
sheep for the burnt offering?"

Abraham said, "Son, God will see to it that
there's a sheep for the burnt offering." And they
kept on walking together.

They arrived at the place to which God had
directed him. Abraham built an altar. He laid
out the wood. Then he tied up Isaac and laid him
on the wood. Abraham reached out and took the
knife to kill his son. (Genesis 22:1-10, MSG)

You know the end of the story on Mt. Moriah — God inter-
vened and provided a ram for the sacrifice. But as Abraham
walked the fifty-mile journey to Moriah, every mile was filled
with anguished questions. *He* did not know the end of the story.

What in the world was going through Abraham's mind?

I think it was something like this. *God, my God, I know your voice,
but could this be you speaking? You say, "TAKE Isaac. GO to Mt. Moriah.
OFFER Isaac on an altar." These are commandments, Lord, not suggestions. Do*

you really mean take, go, offer? The pagans sacrifice their children in fire, but surely you are not asking me to do this. It is against all that you are! You said we were going to worship. This isn't worship. God, I don't understand you — you promised this son long ago to me, and I waited and waited for you to fulfill your promise. Now you ask me to raise a knife and slay my own son? Help, God. HELP!

Abraham was confused, but he still got up early and chopped wood for the altar. He had servants who could have chopped the wood, but it seems that Abraham had to do something physical. With each throw of the ax, he must have inwardly screamed, *Why, God? Why?* Yet he obeyed and said yes to TAKE. GO. OFFER.

Abraham was perplexed, but even though he could not understand God and His ways, Abraham was full of faith. We see his faith in three ways:

1. *Abraham believed that God could raise Isaac from the dead.* His statement, "and we will worship and return to you" (Genesis 22:5) stemmed from his explicit belief in resurrection. We read of his belief in the Faith Hall of Fame in Hebrews 11:17-19.

By faith Abraham offered Isaac as a sacrifice when God was testing him. Abraham, who had received God's promises, was ready to sacrifice his only son, Isaac, even though God had told him, "Isaac is the son through whom your descendants will be counted" (Genesis 21:12, NLT). Abraham reasoned that if Isaac died, God was able to bring him back to life again.

2. *Abraham believed God would provide a lamb.* When Isaac innocently asked, "Daddy, we've got the wood chopped, we have the fire, but we don't have a lamb. Where is the lamb?" (Genesis 22:7, AUTHOR'S PARAPHRASE), his father makes this beautiful proclamation of faith: "God will provide for Himself the lamb for the burnt offering, my son" (verse 8).

3. Abraham trusted God enough to bow. Even though Abraham did not understand what God was doing, he bowed his *intellect*. Even though Abraham loved Isaac with a deep father love, he bowed his *affections*. Even though Abraham wanted to scream, "No, God!" he bowed his *will*.

Abraham's faith statements astonish me. Even though he didn't understand why God was asking him to sacrifice his only son, Abraham looked up and believed. He chose to do God's will and not his own.

We have looked at what was possibly going on in Abraham's mind. But what about the one who was to be sacrificed on an altar?

What in the world was going through Isaac's mind?

Isaac was described as a "lad." The Hebrew word *naar*, which is translated here as "lad," is used in the Old Testament of three-month-old Moses and also of teenagers.[3] Because Isaac was old enough to carry the wood for the altar (see Genesis 22:6), I see him as a young boy about eight years old. As the two journeyed to Mt. Moriah, I imagine that at times Isaac quietly held Abraham's hand and basked in the father-son closeness. Other times he ran and circled his daddy. Isaac delighted in the fact that he was a big enough boy to go with Daddy on this trip. But his excitement turned to terror when the daddy he trusted took the rope and bound *him* to the altar.

Isaac was old enough to know that altars meant fire and death. If you think he quietly went along with being tied to the wood, you don't know young boys. If you had been there on Mt. Moriah, I think you would have heard Isaac scream: "Daddy, Daddy, what are you doing? NO, DADDY! You love me! I'm your boy! NO, DADDY, NO!"

Where was God during this bizarre happening on Mt. Moriah?

What in the world was going through His mind?

Only God knows. The first verse in Genesis 22 says God was testing Abraham. The angel of the Lord revealed that Abraham passed the test with flying colors (see 22:11-12). So God was probably rejoicing. "My servant, Abraham, bows his will to my will, even when he doesn't understand me at all. What a man of faith he is! He is a worshipper of his God."

"Abraham was willing to give up the son he loved to the God who loved him more, and God blessed him. Abraham walked away having experienced God in a way few ever do. God wants to know if we're willing to give up what we love to Him who loves us more. He desires for us to open our fists and trust Him with absolutely everything."[4]

This "giving up" what we love is called *relinquishment*. "It means to let go of, to cease to hold in the hand."[5] It means giving up my rights to control the person, dream, expectation, or preferred outcome of the object of my concern. Relinquishing your "right" to hold your precious Isaac in your own hands is one of the most painful things you will ever do. It seems as irrational as Abraham's decision to place his son on the altar. But when we release our grasp, our relinquishment puts a stop to our manipulation of other people and releases the blessed Holy Spirit to do a supernatural work in our "Isaac."[6]

Transferring our "Isaac" from our hands to God's hands is what we do when we come to the "Isaac altar."

THE ISAAC ALTAR

The first "Isaac altar" was where Abraham stood on Mt. Moriah and bowed his will to God's will. What is an Isaac altar for you and me? It is a place of sacrifice. A place where we choose to yield and not fight. A place where we humbly bow, open our hands, and release our Isaac into God's faithful hands.

Abraham's son Isaac was his beloved child. Your Isaac is someone or something:

You love deeply.

You want deeply.

Like Abraham's, Carol Kent's Isaac was her son. Can you imagine what you would experience if a call from the police in the middle of the night informed you that your godly son was being charged with murder? This is what happened to Carol, author of the deeply honest and faith-inspiring book *When I Lay My Isaac Down* (read this book!). Carol knows about the pain of laying her only son on the altar and bowing her will to God's will. She says:

> True heart sacrifices involve:
>
> * Identifying something precious to us (our Isaac).
> * Letting go of our control over the situation, event, or the person as an act of worship.
> * Embracing God's love in the process of the release.
> * Resting in the outcome, even if in this lifetime we are not allowed to understand the reason behind the need for the sacrifice and the pain involved. [7]

When do we need to build an Isaac altar? Every time something or someone dear to us is threatened or becomes more important to us than the One who first prayed and bowed His will in the garden. But bowing our will in such circumstances is wrenching. It was wrenching for Jesus, for Abraham, for Carol Kent, and it was wrenching for me.

MY ISAAC ALTAR

I had been in this school before. I call it the School of Learning to Bow My Will to God's Will. It's a place where I learn to yield instead of fight. It is not a pleasant place, because my will likes to stand erect instead of bow. I had learned to bow my husband, my children, my home, my friendships, and my ministry to God's will, but on this day I would learn to bow my precious, new granddaughter, Sofia.

It didn't make sense. My daughter, Robin, had lain on her left side for twelve weeks to keep Sofia from being born too soon, but now we learned what the doctors hadn't known previously — Sofia should have been born early. Because of a tear in Robin's placenta, Sofia was born with her skin hanging on her little frame. She had been starving in Robin's womb. My heart screamed, *Oh, God, why? Robin did everything to ensure her daughter was safe.*

I felt helpless. Robin and Sofia were in Finland; I was in Colorado. The phone calls were pain-filled: "Mom, Sofia must have another blood transfusion. I feel so guilty, Mom. I should have known there was something wrong."

I walked out to my rock sanctuary behind my home, knowing that I must surrender my mind, my heart, and my will. Abraham had to surrender these three things and so did I. I had to bow:

- *My intellect* — I had to bow my understanding. My daughter had been through much illness and had waited for this precious child for many years. I had to affirm that I would trust in the Lord with all my heart and lean not on my own understanding. (see Proverbs 3:5)
- *My affections* — I had never seen my new granddaughter, Sofia, but I loved her with a deep "Nana love." I had to surrender my emotions.
- *My will* — I wanted my granddaughter to live and be healthy and happy. I longed for her to develop physically and intellectually in a normal way. But I had to will to do the will of God in preference to my own will.[8]

Abraham went to Mt. Moriah in obedience. He went in worship. He went in faith and built his altar. I had to build my altar with tears and trembling hands, with the hands of my heart. This was my worship. So among the rocks behind my house, I knelt on a soft cushion of pine needles and opened my hands to God. I meditated on this verse: "Because the Sovereign LORD helps me, I will not be disgraced. Therefore, I have set my face like a stone [flint], determined to do his will. And I know that I will not be put to shame" (Isaiah 50:7, NLT). Then I prayed:

> *My Father, right now I lift my precious, new granddaughter to you. She is yours. I trust her to you. I ask you humbly for her life. Oh, God, rescue her! Save her! Protect her! I beg you to keep her from harm. But, my Lord, I lift Sofia and bind her with the hands of my heart to the Isaac altar. I bow my will to your will. Receive it, precious Lord, as my worship.*

If you had been in my rock sanctuary that day, you would know I whispered my prayer through deep sobs.

My Isaac was someone I loved deeply. Jean's Isaac was very different.

JEAN'S ISAAC ALTAR

Have you ever received a letter or email so touching that you spent hours thinking about it? I have. It was an email from Jean Baumgardner, received on April 24, 2002.

Her words began:

> Because of our certain confidence in God's good-ness and grace, John, Christina, and I want to give Him thanks for the way He is ordering our lives. Today we met with my primary care doctor and discussed a number of issues including ways I might boost my energy level, hospice care, and

pain management. Her prognosis for my life expectancy was two to four weeks because of how rapidly my liver is failing.

My thoughts began: *This is amazing. Jean is dying. She is a relatively young woman in her forties. Her daughter, Christina, is a college student. Jean will miss growing old with the husband she loves. She will miss the joy of planning and attending her only child's wedding. She will miss knowing her grandchildren. Yet, she is offering God thanks for the way He is ordering her life . . . and her death. She is bowing her will to His will, just as Jesus did.*

Jean's email continued:

Given my present circumstances, I would like to share some of my thoughts on death with you. I began a relationship with the Lord Jesus when I was eight years old. I have known Him as my Creator, my Redeemer, my Friend, my Sustainer, and the One who gives me value and worth. I have lived my entire life conscious and grateful for the eternal life He granted me. I have long realized this life is short, but eternity is long, and have looked forward to being with Him in that place He promised to be preparing for me.

I am persuaded that God determines the time, place, and manner in which a believer dies. I believe the Lord Jesus demonstrated His triumph over death and the grave, and that in belonging to Him, I too am a partaker in that same triumph. Although it is sad to be separated for a while from those I love, my trust in Jesus gives me comfort and strength.

My prayer is that you also have truly put your trust in Jesus, and Him alone, for your eternal

destiny and that we will be able to rejoice forever
and ever together.

My thoughts continue: *Jean is dying and the longing of her heart is to share the joy of knowing Jesus with everyone she knows. I see that Jean can bow her will because she bowed every part of her life first.*

Jean's email touched me deeply, but her P.S. caused me to spend hours in prayer and meditation:

> P.S.
> Learn your lines! What do I mean by this? For the last two months I've been memorizing all the verses in Revelation that are songs we will be singing to God and to the Lamb around the throne. I want to show up prepared. Join me!

My thoughts on Jean's P.S.: *Oh God, I am humbled. I long to be a worshipper like Jean. I long to bow my knee, my life, my will to you.*

Abraham placed his son on the altar. I placed my grand-daughter on the altar. Jean lifted her very life and placed it on the altar and said, "I bow my will to your will." Perhaps you are asking, "But how do I believe and bow my will when the lights of understanding have gone out, when my life is crumbled hope and shattered dreams?" The answer is wrapped up in the word *Jireh,* which means "provision."

In Genesis 22:14 we read that Abraham renamed the mountain of sacrifice. Mt. Moriah became "The LORD Will Provide." A place of deep sorrow became Jehovah-Jireh, "The LORD Will Provide."

Abraham's provision was the ram caught in the thicket (see Genesis 22:13). I find it interesting that Abraham didn't see or hear the ram, which is a large animal, until he had bowed his will to God's will. We have a Colorado version of a "thicket" around our home. It is a dense, tall bush called scrub oak. When our big dog walks through the scrub oak, you can easily hear him. I am convinced that God's provision for Abraham, the ram, had always been there, asleep in the thicket. God's provision was there when Abraham built the altar. God's provision was there when Abraham tied Isaac to the wood and lifted the knife. Through it all, God's provision of the ram was there!

In the same way, God plants His provision for *you* in the midst of your crisis. You cannot see it. But it is there! Jehovah-Jireh is your personal God who provides your "ram."

My friend, I think you know what I'm going to ask you now, don't you?

COME, LET'S GET PRACTICAL

It is time for you to go before your Father God and ask Him to give you the courage and strength to build your own Isaac altar.

1. *Ask yourself, "Who or what is my Isaac?"* Is it your grandchild? Is it your life? Is it your child, your marriage, your grown child who is no longer a child but acting like one? Is it your ambition, health, finances, security, or gifts?

2. *Read the story of the Isaac altar in Genesis 22:1-18.* Ask God to give you deep understanding as you read.

3. *Find a place to be alone with the Lord and bow in worship.* Still your heart before God. Tell Him that you have come to build your altar with tears and trembling hands.

4. *Lay your Isaac on the altar.*

    ✦ Pray a prayer like this: My Father, right now I give
      _____ to you. He is yours. I trust him
      to you. I lift_____ and bind him with
      the hands of my heart to the Isaac altar. I bow my will
      to your will. Receive it, precious Lord, as my worship.

    ✦ Act out your relinquishment by imagining yourself
      lifting _____to the altar and binding
      him to the wood.

Do you long to be a Trusting One? Will you let God be God?
Will you lay your Isaac on the altar of your heart? Will you choose
to bow your will and worship your great and awesome God? It is
the deepest act of worship!

Chapter 12

—

Drawn into His Presence

Chapter 12

Drawn into His Presence

For He has satisfied the thirsty soul,

and the hungry soul He has filled with what is good.

PSALM 107:9

A monk in the 1600s experienced it.

A nineteen-year-old soldier in Bornea during WWII experienced it.

A missionary in the Philippines in 1941 experienced it.

Women in the twenty-first century are experiencing it.

I am experiencing it!

What is "it"?

It is the cool drink of water that quenches our restless spirit and satisfies our thirsty soul.

It is the answer to our cry for sweet face-to-face intimacy.

It is the presence of God.

For many years, I had longed to experience God's presence in a deeper, more tangible way. I remember the first time I read *The Practice of the Presence of God* by Brother Lawrence. This wise monk claimed one could walk in God's presence all day long. My spirit soared: *Yes, God, yes! This is what I want — to experience your presence every moment of every day!* The same thing happened the first time I read Thomas Kelly's *A Testament of Devotion* and learned that it was possible to live on two levels (the spiritual level and the physical level) at once. This learned Quaker theologian said that deep worship and prayer could go on while one is active about the business of life. My spirit soared again when I read the journal of Frank Laubach, a missionary who yearned deeply for the presence of God like a panting deer thirsts for a waterbrook. Like Brother Lawrence and Kelly, Laubach discovered deep joy as he learned the secrets of abiding moment by moment in God's presence.

But although I longed for what these three men described, I found myself dismissing their words. After all, Brother Lawrence was a monk living in a monastery. Kelly was a theologian who spent endless hours immersed in God's Word. And Frank Laubach went up on a mountaintop for two years to seek God's presence. My thoughts countered: *Wow — maybe I could discover God's presence too if I spent all my time in a monastery, or studying the Bible, or living secluded on a mountaintop. But that's not real life. Besides my writing and speaking ministry, I've got a husband to please, four kids to cart all over town, a house to clean, and twenty-one meals to prepare every week! Come on, gentlemen! Show me how it's possible to experience God's presence while I'm washing another load of dirty socks.*

The question I posed to myself was this: I want what these men have, but how do I get there? What does it look like for me, a woman in the twenty-first century, to walk in God's presence? Like Brother Lawrence, could I turn my thoughts back to God — even while I was struggling to balance my checkbook? Like Thomas Kelly, could I live on the spiritual level of worshipping God — even while shuttling teenagers to sports activities? Like Frank Laubach, could I experience the sweet abiding presence of God — even in the midst of a book deadline?

YES! I say, Yes! Slowly, ever so slowly, I have experienced God's presence in a real way. Even while I was outwardly busy with activities and chores, I recognized a growing inward delight as I took my mind continually back to God. How did this happen?

In the beginning of this book I told you that the secret longing of every heart is face-to-face intimacy. Then I shared how the yearning for intimacy can be satisfied through worship. I explained that worship:

> begins in holy expectancy
> ends in holy obedience

And now, the grand surprise — worship ushers us into the presence of God. *Hidden in worship is His presence.*

The experience of God's presence far surpasses any pleasure or treasure to be found on earth. In God's presence are found peace and fullness of joy. As educator Peter Rowe writes, God's presence is "home."[1]

Rowe goes on to say that "You cannot divorce God from His presence any more than you can experience my presence without me. The presence of God is not just a feeling, nor is it like a fragrance that can be enjoyed at a distance from a flower. The presence of God is GOD HIMSELF; His presence has substance. All spirit has substance — the spirit realm is very real."[2]

God's Word gives us guidance about what God's presence looks and feels like. In God's presence we experience:

- joy (Isaiah 9:3; Acts 2:28)
- refreshment (Acts 3:19)
- rest (Psalm 46:10; Exodus 33:14)
- help (Psalm 42:5)
- pleasure (Psalm 16:11)

Talking about the presence of God fills me with anticipation, so I am excited to come to this last chapter. But before I share with you what God is teaching me about His presence, and the joy that comes from this type of face-to-face intimacy, I want us to review all that we have learned, so think back with me through the chapters of this book and consider the questions I ask you.

Chapter 1 shows how worship was my path to discover face-to-face intimacy. When you read this did you say, "Yes, Lord, I want to grow as a worshipper," or did you say, "No"?

Chapter 2 was about my worship awakening and growing in awe, astonished wonder, and adoration. Was your response, "Yes, Lord, teach me. Awaken my heart to worship?" Or did you say, "Not interested"?

Chapter 3 was all about quieting your restless soul. Did you say, "I long to discover stillness," or did you say, "That just isn't me"?

Chapter 4 shows you five of my worship experiences. Did you read with open ears and an open heart, or were you closed to new thoughts?

Chapter 5 When you read about laying your life on the altar as your spiritual act of worship, did you shout, "Amen," or did you turn your heart away?

Chapter 6 To bow your words as an act of worship is so hard! But what was your response? Did you determine to bless and not curse those you love or did you walk away?

Chapter 7 Bowing your attitude may have caused more squirming. Did you say, "Yes, Lord, I choose to have an attitude of gratitude"?

Chapter 8 Did you get excited when you learned that your work can be worship? Did you make a *"Laborare est Orare. Orare est Laborare"* plaque or did you think, "This is silly"?

Chapter 9 To bow your times of waiting can be agonizing. Did you tell God, "My times are in your hands," or did you look the other way?

Chapter 10 If you are in pain, you know that bowing

> your pain is excruciating. Did you make a secret
> choice to bow your pain or did you tune out?
> *Chapter 11* The deepest worship is to bow your
> will to God's will. Did you build an Isaac altar
> or say, "No way"?

Why did I take you through this review? Because every "Yes, Lord" you said, every secret choice you made to bow before your Father God, is a step toward intimacy with Him.

We've looked back; now let's look forward and consider how scheduling appointments with God will take us a step closer to greater intimacy. Discover what surprise encounters look like and how sweet continual communion with God is possible!

SCHEDULED APPOINTMENTS

Does scheduling times with God sound slightly robotic? Does it take away the mystery for you? Believe me, I am not talking about having a mechanical encounter with God. Tomorrow morning I have scheduled an appointment with the Lover of my soul. I am going to meet with Him.

> *Think* anticipation
> *Think* adventure
> *Think* awe

Did you get what I just said? *I have the privilege of fellowshipping with the Creator of the universe!* He — the Almighty, Majestic One — invites me to share a meal with Him! "Look! I stand at the door and knock. If you hear my voice and open the door, I will come in, and we will share a meal together as friends" (Revelation 3:20, NLT).

Perhaps, like me, you have only seen this verse as an invitation to receive Christ as Savior. If you look closely at the context, you will see that these words are written to a church. It is an invitation to intimacy. This is not duty, but delight.

So, what is a scheduled appointment with God?

It is Jesus praying through the night in an olive grove. It is Jesus getting on a boat to be alone with His Father. It is Mary of Bethany sitting at Jesus' feet to learn, to weep, and to worship Him. It is David panting, hungering, and thirsting for the Lord, earnestly seeking Him. It is David saying the one thing he seeks is to dwell in the house of the Lord all the days of his life and behold the beauty of the Lord (see Psalm 27:4).

It is not just men and women in the Bible. It is *you* getting on your knees and saying, "Lord, teach me to worship you!" It is *you* praying about bowing your times of waiting before God.

It is purposeful pursuit of Him.

It is intentional intimacy with Him.

You are purposeful and intentional when you have a daily "quiet time," when you practice the Twenty-Minute Worship Experience, and when you read and study this book. When you commit to do the twelve-week Bible study at the end of this book, when you write in the accompanying journal, you are saying, "I want to grow as a worshipper. I long to experience face-to-face intimacy with God!"

I remember as a new believer being told, "Linda, if you had an appointment with the president of the United States, you wouldn't be late. Well, every morning, Linda, you have an appointment with the God of the universe. Could anything be more important?" It made sense to this college student, and so I began the practice of opening my Bible every morning in what my new friends called a "quiet time."

My scheduled appointments with my Lord have changed as I've moved from being a servant to a worshipper. Previously, my time was ordered primarily by my mind and learning God's Word. Now, I've added my heart and adoring Him in worship.

During the past week I've recorded all the set appointments and impromptu meetings I've had with the Lord.

- I began the week by pulling on my snow boots and strapping on my iPod. Then I took a holy hike amid the newly fallen snow and worshipped the Holy One.
- Early in the mornings, I met with the Lord as I opened my Bible. Sometimes I read the Psalms on my knees and personalized them back to God.
- I waited in silence on my knees before God, listening to His voice.
- I had three phone appointments to pray with women over the phone — these were appointments with God and a woman.
- As I rode the recumbent bike in our basement, I worshipped and prayed.
- I worshipped and prayed with my friend Becky.
- I worshipped with my husband at a church service.
- I woke in the middle of the night and went to my office and worshipped on my knees.
- Yesterday while talking to a friend on the phone, we spontaneously began praying for a mutual friend in pain. It was a precious time — the Holy Spirit was alive through the phone lines.
- I put on a Christmas CD (it's November so I thought it was permissible) and ended up on my knees thanking my God for sending Jesus.
- During a conversation with my husband, my tongue became a "wild animal," and I fell to my knees confessing and asking the Holy One to take me deeper in bowing my words in worship.
- When I had no wisdom for the outline for this chapter, I put on soft worship music and waited on my knees in stillness for God to give His wisdom.

I have also had three-day and four-day scheduled encounters with God, but Moses had a forty-day appointment with God on Mt. Sinai. I am sure that this time of fasting included much waiting. We know Moses waited for six days in the cloud cover before God called him to come higher up the mountain on the seventh day (see Exodus 24:16-17). When Moses walked higher, he experienced a surprise encounter with the Holy One; he beheld the manifest presence of the Lord.

As I purposely pursued the Holy One, I began to sense His presence in my scheduled times of worship. Scheduled appointments open up the possibility of surprise encounters.

SURPRISE ENCOUNTERS

As we journey to a place of deeper intimacy with God, He may come to us in special ways.

> *Think* unexpected
> *Think* enveloped
> *Think* overwhelmed

As we talk about encounters with God, keep in mind these three important truths:

- We cannot make these surprise encounters happen.
- We should always seek God Himself and not an experience.
- God chooses how to meet each unique person, and one kind of encounter with God is not "more spiritual" than another.

In a scheduled appointment, I take the initiative. I am purposeful and intentional. I come to meet with my loving Father.

In a surprise encounter, God comes to meet with me. It's as if the roles are reversed. As amazing as it sounds, God is purposeful in His pursuit of me! He longs for intentional intimacy with me! Come with me as I share surprise encounters that I and other worshippers have experienced.

My Car Encounter

It was an ordinary day doing an ordinary errand — picking up a friend from the airport. On the drive back to my friend's home, I pushed in a worship CD and we spontaneously began to worship. Since I was driving, I refrained from closing my eyes and raising both my hands, but this did not prevent my spirit from soaring with delight as together we sang praise to our Father. About midway into a particularly beautiful song, a heavy presence filled the car — heavy not in the sense of weight but in the sense that the air was charged with the tangible glory of God. It filled the car like a cloud. Neither of us said anything, we knew it at the same time, without saying a word. We were both undone. I don't even remember pulling off the road, but I must have, because the next thing I remember was being at the side of the road. The glory of God's presence took my breath away as we sat in stunned silence.

I do not pretend to understand why God came at this moment. I don't even have the ability to accurately describe within the confines of words what that experience meant to me. All I know is that God's manifest presence is very real, that He shows up at very unpredictable times, and that when He does, it produces in me a joy like no other.

A "Quiet Time" Encounter

Brenda, a single woman: During a time of worship, I felt the Lord's hand cupping my face and lifting my head. In my heart, He spoke these words: "Dance with me; dance with your Husband."

Prompted by His voice, I began worshipping Him, twirling and spinning around the floor. I was beside myself, rejoicing, singing, and weeping, all at once.

On that day, the Lord knew that I was carrying around a certain heaviness, so He opened my eyes to see there was *no* lack in my life that He wouldn't go out of His way to fill.[3]

A Phone Encounter

I often pray over women on the phone, so when I dialed the number in Idaho, I was not expecting a surprise encounter with the Lord. Yet as I prayed, it was as if a heavy cloud surrounded me. The glory of God descended in such a tangible way, I finally had to get off the phone and just bask in the sweet silence of His presence. An email the next day told me that the dear woman on the other end of the line felt the same heavy presence in her car.

Why did God give a surprise encounter over the phone? I do not know. I just praised Him.

An Early Morning Encounter

My friend Lorraine and I were staying in a motel room in Texas, as we had an Intimate Issues Conference that weekend. For some reason, we both woke up at 5 a.m. and began to share about how we heard God's voice. As we lay in our beds talking about the Lord, we were enveloped by the visible cloud of God's presence. Our talking ceased. It seemed as if sleeping crystals were dropped on us as we both fell asleep instantly and were awakened together an hour later. The holiness was still present and we couldn't speak. We stayed in the sweet silence, just enjoying the pleasure of His company. Such a holiness was present in the room that we could not talk about what we had experienced, and we had no idea what it meant.

A month later we talked about the beauty of this divine encounter and discovered the Lord had revealed to us both the purpose of this encounter. It was so precious that we have never been able to speak of it.

A Cabin Encounter

Pat: When I first walked into the prayer cabin, I sensed the presence of the Lord there. I climbed up into the loft and delighted in the view of the handiwork of the God of creation. My time at the cabin was limited, so I began to pray earnestly. I whispered, *Lord, I feel that I scarcely know you, but I want to know you much better. The more I know you, the more I realize how very little I truly know you. I want to see you. I want to sense your presence. I want to be like you, and I want to be with you.* God's presence poured over me like liquid love. I sensed, in a very tangible way, the nature of His unconditional love for me.

When asked if this encounter with God is

> a learned experience, Pat says, No. But what she
> says is learned is yielding.[4]

You have been learning about yielding, as it is a key message of this book. Most of the chapters are titled, "I Bow_____" (my words, work, and so on). When we bow a particular aspect of our life to God, we are yielding it to Him.

Scheduled appointments with my Father open up the possibility of surprise encounters with Him. As I consistently and intentionally pursue set meetings with my Beloved, He occasionally envelops me in a surprise encounter with Him. Both kinds of encounters with God can lead to sweet communion with Him.

SWEET COMMUNION

> *Think* abiding
> *Think* continual
> *Think* steady

Come with me and learn from Brother Lawrence, Frank Laubach, and Thomas Kelly, the three men who first made my soul thirsty for God's presence. These men lived in different centuries and different countries, yet each possessed a deep hunger to discover the practical presence of God.

Brother Lawrence

Over the years, I have repeatedly read *The Practice of the Presence of God*. Each time my spirit would sigh with longing. I yearned for what Brother Lawrence had. He was ever thinking delightful thoughts of God, holding love for the Lord in his heart — I yearned for the way he walked and talked with God. God's presence was his daily reality. He made some amazing statements:[5]

- ❧ "I have no will but that of God."
- ❧ "I make it my business only to continue in His holy presence."
- ❧ "I have a habitual, silent, and secret conversation of the soul with God."
- ❧ "I desire God to make His perfect image in my soul and change me entirely like Him."
- ❧ "I desire only Him and want to be wholly devoted to Him."

Dear Brother Lawrence, wanting to share his own experience with the presence of God, yet wanting to be humble, talks of his spiritual walk in the third person.

> I know a person who for forty years has practiced the presence of God, to which he gives several other names. Sometimes he calls it a simple act — a clear and distinct knowledge of God; and sometimes he calls it a vague view of a general and loving look at God — a remembrance of Him. He also refers to it as attention to God, silent communion with God, confidence in God, or the life and the peace of the soul.
>
> To sum it up, this person has told me that all these manners of the presence of God are synonyms which signify the same thing, which have all become natural to him. The presence of God is the concentration of the soul's attention on God, remembering that He is always present.
>
> My friend says that by dwelling in the presence of God he has established such a sweet communion with the Lord that His spirit abides,

without much effort, in the restful peace of God. In this rest, he is filled with faith that equips him to handle anything that comes to him.

This is what he calls the "actual presence" of God, which includes any and all kinds of communion a person who still dwells on the earth can possibly have with God in heaven. At times, he can live as if no one else existed on earth but himself and God. He lovingly speaks with God wherever he goes, asking Him for all he needs and rejoicing with Him in a thousand ways.[6]

Dear Brother Lawrence said he had a habitual sense of God's presence. After this monk filled his mind, through prayer, with great thoughts of God, he went to his appointed work in the monastery kitchen. He planned each thing that needed to be done to prepare the meal, and then said to God with devoted trust in Him:

In obedience to Your commands, as I apply my mind to these outward things, I ask You to grant me the grace to continue in Your presence. To this end make me prosper through Your assistance. Receive all my work, and possess all my affections.[7]

For Brother Lawrence, it was all about knowing God intimately. February 6, 1691, he wrote, "I hope, by His mercy, for the privilege of seeing Him face to face within a few days."[8] Several days after penning these thoughts, Brother Lawrence died and entered into face-to-face intimacy forever.

Two hundred years later, another worshipper longed to abide in God's presence. His name was Frank Laubach.

Frank Laubach

At the age of forty-five, this missionary to the Philippines began the practice of abiding in the presence of Christ. It has been said that Frank Laubach lived one of the fullest lives ever lived by one of Christ's followers. He wrote over fifty books, was known as a great educator of modern times, yet he is remembered for letters written from a shack on Signal Hill on the island of Mindanao. In these letters written to his father, Frank details his search for the presence of God.[9]

March 23, 1930

One question now to be put to the test is this: Can we have that contact with God all the time? All the time awake, fall asleep in His arms, and awaken in His presence? Can we attain that? Can we do His will all the time? Can we think His thoughts all the time?[10]

September 29, 1930

When God gave His presence, he wrote, "It is difficult to convey to another the joy of having broken into the new sea of realizing God's 'hereness.' It seemed so wonderfully true that just the privilege of fellowship with God is infinitely more than anything God could give. When He gives Himself He is giving more than anything else in the universe."[11]

October 12, 1930

How I wish, wish, wish that a dozen or more persons who are trying to hold God endlessly in mind would all write their experiences so that each would know what the other was finding as a result! The results, I think, would astound the world. At least the results of my own effort are astounding to me. . . . The very universe has come to seem so homey! I know only a little more about it than before, but that little is all! It is vibrant with the electric ecstasy of God! I know what it means to be "God intoxicated."[12]

Thomas Kelly

Thomas Kelly and Frank Laubach were contemporaries. Like Brother Lawrence and Laubach, Thomas Kelly, in *A Testament of Devotion*, put words to his practice of the presence of God.

There is a way of ordering our mental life on more than one level at once. On one level we may be thinking, discussing, seeing, calculating, meeting all the demands of external affairs. But deep within, behind the scenes, at a profounder level, we may also be in prayer and adoration, song and worship and a gentle receptiveness to divine breathings.[13]

When I first read his *A Testament of Devotion*, my heart leaped, as Kelly had put words to what I was beginning to experience. I cried, "Yes, yes, it is possible to live on two levels. I am discovering this as I live a lifestyle of worship!" I will be in my kitchen (like Brother Lawrence) cooking for missionaries or writing at my desk (like Thomas Kelly), my mind on "outward" things, but when I turn inward, where my Lord resides, it is as if I've never left. I am aware that worship has been going on from my spirit to Him who is Spirit while I was cooking and writing! Oh, it is so beautiful to be aware of the continuous connection, spirit-to-Spirit.

I had longed to experience God's abiding presence, to know continual spirit-to-Spirit communion, and I found it happening as I walked out my worship. I shouldn't have been surprised as Psalm 89:15 (NLT) promises: "Happy are those who hear the joyful call to worship, for they will walk in the light of your presence, LORD."

Worship is my pathway to discovering deep intimacy in God's presence. Practicing God's presence and living on two levels is a process — an exciting process. I pray that as you have read this book you can say, "My thirsty soul *is* being satisfied as I am growing as a worshipper." You are growing and I am continuing to grow too!

So, I begin my days on my knees — I bow my knee to the only One who is worthy. I love Him, I adore Him, and I bow my life once again — every aspect of my life. I worship and serve as I walk in the light of His presence. He is ever near and I am near to Him. My thoughts continually return to Him, and when they do, my heart leaps with joy. It's as if I've never left — my spirit has continued to rejoice before Him as I've been briefly occupied with my everyday earthly existence.

Daily as I come into His presence, this is my prayer:

> *My Father, today I long to walk my worship before You.*
> *Therefore:*
> *I bow my knees,*
> *I bow my words,*
> *I bow my work,*
> *I bow my attitude,*
> *I bow my times of waiting,*
> *I bow my pain,*

I bow my will.
I bow my life to you as my spiritual act of worship.

One day the emphasis of my prayer will be my attitude, another day my words. I see my life before my Lord as a moving picture, ready to be lived out in the twenty-four hours given. As I walk through the hours, lifting my words, my work, every facet of my being, to Him as an act of worship, *I am drawn into His presence.*

I pray you will be too!

Twelve-Week

Bible Study

for

—

Satisfy My Thirsty Soul

BIBLE STUDY FOR

Satisfy My Thirsty Soul

Dear Friend,

I'm very excited that you have chosen to grow as a worshipper! You have taken a step forward by reading *Satisfy My Thirsty Soul.* Working through this twelve-week Bible study is an important second step. An attractive companion journal, *My Worship Journey*, accompanies this book. The journal has been created so you have a place to record your own personal journey as a worshipper.

There are four parts to each week's study:

- ❧ Delving into God's Word
- ❧ Memorizing and meditating on Scripture
- ❧ Practicing worship experiences
- ❧ Reflecting on what you are learning

Delving into God's Word

Each week you will study passages of Scripture and answer questions that will teach you truths about a lifestyle of worship. Record your answers in this book.

Memorizing and Meditating on Scripture

Studying God's Word is good, but *memorizing* and *meditating* on Scripture will place His Word in your heart and mind. As you store God's Word and His wisdom in your heart, you will be changed.

Each week you'll be encouraged to memorize two verses. If this seems like too much, select one verse and learn it well. Then use the verse (or verses) to praise God. Pray the verse back to Him. Here is an example of how you might do that with one of the verses from the first week's study.

- ❧ *Verse*: "Happy are those who hear the joyful call to worship, for they will walk in the light of your presence, LORD." (Psalm 89:15, NLT)
- ❧ *My Praise*: My Lord, thank you for this wonderful promise. You say that I will become filled with joy as I grow as a worshipper. I praise you that I will walk in the glorious light of your presence!
- ❧ *My Prayer*: My Father, I long for this promise to become a reality in my life. Teach me, Holy Spirit, how to hear the call to worship. Make me sensitive to your voice. I ask you that I would discover all it means to walk in the light of your presence.

Practicing Worship Experiences

I encourage you — I *strongly* encourage you — to practice private worship each week. I encourage you to try both the ABCs of Worship (see pages 47-48) and the Twenty-Minute Worship Experience (see page 68). Write down your thoughts and feelings as you grow as a worshipper. (*My Worship Journey* journal has a place for you to do this each week. You will need a journal. If you do not purchase *My Worship Journey*, find another journal to use.)

Reflecting on What You Are Learning

As you learn from God's Word and from practicing the worship experiences, it's helpful to reflect on what you are learning about God, worship, and yourself. Again, *My Worship Journey* journal has places for you to write your reflections each week.

As I've grown as a worshipper, I have been changed. I have experienced God's very real presence and my relationship with Him has become deep and satisfying. I am praying that as you do this study, you will grow in intimacy with the Lord!

Linda Dillow

WEEK 1

My Thirsty Soul

1. Read chapter 1, "My Thirsty Soul," two times.

2. Write Psalm 89:15 and Psalm 16:11 here. Then store them up in your mind by memorizing them.

3. In what ways do women search for intimacy? Where have you searched?

4. Write a paragraph describing what face-to-face intimacy with God looks like to you.

5. Read Matthew 22:37-39.

   a. Do you think women tend to get these two commandments mixed up?

   b. Have you mixed them up, and if so, explain what that
       looked like in your life.

6. Can you say, "This is who I am. I am not primarily a
    worker for God. I am first and foremost a lover of God"?
    What does it mean to you to be a "lover of God"?

7. Read and meditate on Ephesians 5:31-32. How does it make
    you feel that God says sexual intimacy in marriage is a
    picture of the degree of spiritual intimacy that He longs to
    have with us?

8. Read Exodus chapters 19, 20, and 24.

   a. Read the description of "Levels of Intimacy" on pages
       21-22.
   b. Which circle are you in now? Where would you like to
       be?

9. Read Philippians 3:13-14; Psalm 27:4; and Luke 10:41-42.

   a. What is the "one thing" you choose?

   b. Write a prayer to God about your choice.

10. Paraphrase Psalm 63:1-8.

11. Read Psalm 29:1-2. It is called the biblical definition of worship. Use these verses to write out how you would explain worship to a child.

12. Which of the following definitions of worship do you like the best? Why?

   ❧ "Worship is the outpouring of a soul at rest in the presence of God." — A. P. Gibbs

   ❧ "Worship is a way of gladly reflecting back to God the radiance of His worth." — John Piper

❧ "Worship is giving God the best that He has given you." — Oswald Chambers

❧ "Worship is the overflow of a grateful heart, under a sense of Divine favor." — A. P. Gibbs

13. Write your definition of worship in one to two sentences.

14. What do these two statements say to you?

   a. Worship is a specific act where I declare, "Holy, Holy, Holy."

   b. Worship is a lifestyle where I live "Holy, Holy, Holy."

Now, take out your journal and record your answers to these questions.

15. What did you learn about God this week?

16. What did you learn about worship this week?

17. What did you learn about yourself this week?

18. Write a prayer of thanksgiving to God to express what you learned.

WEEK 2

My Worship Awakening

1. Read chapter 2, "My Worship Awakening," two times.

2. Memorize two verses (or more) from 1 Chronicles 29:11-14. Write your memory verses here.

3. Read Isaiah 6:1-8 as if you've never read it before.

   a. Describe what Isaiah saw when he looked *upward* (6:1-4).

   b. Describe what Isaiah saw when he looked *inward* (6:5-6).

   c. Describe what Isaiah saw when he looked *outward* (6:7-8).

   d. Have you ever had an upward — inward — outward experience with the Lord? If so, what did God teach you?

   e. Have you ever asked God to strike you with the awe of His holiness?

4. Read Psalm 95:6. What does it look like for you to bow before your God?

5. Explain this statement: "When I bow, I submit my sense of superiority because to worship is to acknowledge an inferior before a superior."

6. Read Psalm 96; Psalm 97:1-6; and Psalm 98:1-8.

   a. Go on a half-hour to hour walk. (If it is 105 degrees or 25 degrees, take a fast walk!) If possible, sit quietly and ask God to fill you with astonished wonder over His creation. Observe. Relax. Enjoy. Feel the wind and the sun. Watch the clouds.

254 SATISFY MY THIRSTY SOUL

b. Take your journal with you and record anything you see or that God whispers to you through His creation.

c. Read Psalm 19:1-4. Go outside at night and look at the heavens. Ask God to give you childlike wonder and awe.

7. Have you ever thought about your spirit having senses? How can your spiritual senses be quickened through use?

8. Ponder these words of A. P. Gibbs: "In prayer we are occupied with our needs, in thanksgiving we are occupied with our blessings, but in worship we are totally occupied with God Himself."

a. What does this quote say to you?

b. How can you be totally occupied with God Himself?

9. What do A. W. Tozer's words about adoring God (see pages 45-46) say to you?

10. The Hebrew (Old Testament) word for *worship* means "to fall prostrate." The Greek (New Testament) word for *worship* means "to kiss toward."

    a. What does the Hebrew word imply about worship?

    b. What does the Greek word imply about worship?

    c. What do you see as the difference between the two meanings?

11. What does it look like for you to adore God?

12. Kneel, stand, or take a walk and worship the Holy One by going through the ABCs of Worship. Record in your journal anything God shows you about Himself.

Now, take out your journal and record your answers to these questions.

13. What did you learn about God this week?

14. What did you learn about worship this week?

15. What did you learn about yourself this week?

16. Write a prayer of thanksgiving to God to express what you learned.

WEEK 3

My Soul Finds Stillness

1. Read chapter 3, "My Soul Finds Stillness," two times.

2. Memorize Psalm 46:10 and Psalm 131:2. Write your memory verses here.

3. Practice the Twenty-Minute Worship Experience. Spend ten to twenty minutes a day in private worship. If possible, be on your knees (yes, you can use a pillow). Journal daily about your worship time. Here are some suggestions for your worship time:

   a. Pray Psalm 131, asking God to reveal to you how your soul can be stilled.

   b. Put on a headset and worship with worship music. Sing or say the music to God.

   c. Read prayerfully the songs of worship from Revelation 4 and 5.

4. Write your own personal "prayer of quiet." If you like, use Richard Foster's prayer as a guide (see page 64). Pray your "prayer of quiet" every day this week.

5. Read Psalm 46 twice. Read it in another translation than you normally use.

   a. What does verse 10 add to this rich psalm?

   b. How does "being still" lead to knowing God is exalted in all the earth?

6. What does external clamor and internal chaos look like in your life? What helps you to stop the clamor and chaos that assault you? List as many things as you can think of.

7. Read Psalm 131. Paraphrase this little psalm.

8. Read Luke 10:38-42; Luke 7; and John 12:1-7.

   Make two lists, a Martha list and a Mary list. As you read the above passages, ask God to show you every attribute of these two women.

   Martha   Mary

Now, take out your journal and record your answers to these questions.

9. What did you learn about God this week?

10. What did you learn about yourself this week?

11. What did you learn about worship this week?

WEEK 4

Expanding My Worship Experience

1. Read chapter 4, "Expanding My Worship Experience," two times.

2. Memorize John 4:23-24. Write the verses here.

3. Practice the Twenty-Minute Worship Experience. Spend ten to twenty minutes a day in private worship. Suggestions for this time:

   a. Personalize Psalm 95 and pray it to the Lord.

   b. Read prayerfully Revelation 19:1-16.

4. What were your thoughts after reading about Linda's five worship experiences (pages 71-73)? Where do you worship?

5. Write your own version of the Lord's Prayer.

6. Read John 4:1-42. Write a synopsis of the interaction between Jesus and the Samaritan woman. Include whatever you feel is important.

7. Review John 4:23-24 about worshipping in truth — to worship in truth is to worship *truly*. This means you must know God's Word and be sincere.

   a. How are you filling your mind and heart consistently with God's Word so that you can worship in truth?

   b. What can you do to add to your current knowledge of God's Word?

c. Are you coming to God totally transparent, or are you wearing a mask? Explain your answer.

8. Review John 4:23-24 about worshipping in spirit — to worship in spirit is to worship *spiritually*. This means you must be spiritual.

   a. Ask God to search your heart as you meditate and pray Psalm 19:12-14 and Psalm 139:23-24. Write down anything God reveals to you.

   b. What does it look like for you to worship by the power of the Holy Spirit?

9. Write a paragraph describing your thoughts and feelings after you read "I Saw Joni Dance" (see pages 81-83).

10. Pages 83-85 list four practical suggestions for how you can begin to worship God in spirit and in truth. (1) Ask God to give you a picture of who He is. (2) Search out special places to worship. (3) Find music that lifts your spirit, and allow it to lead you in worship. (4) Give yourself permission to express your worship.

   a. Which of these four suggestions are you already including in your private worship, and how have they encouraged you?

   b. Which of the four suggestions would you like to consider adding to your worship? How can you make that happen?

Now, take out your journal and record your answers to these questions.

11. What did you learn about God this week?

12. What did you learn about worship this week?

13. What did you learn about yourself this week?

WEEK 5

I Bow My Life

1. Read chapter 5, "I Bow My Life," two times.

2. Memorize Romans 12:1 and John 14:21.

   a. Write these verses here.

   b. Write your own personalized version of Romans 12:1 and John 14:21 here.

3. Practice the Twenty-Minute Worship Experience. Spend ten to twenty minutes a day in private worship. Suggestions for your worship time:

   a. Personalize Psalm 139 and pray it to the Lord.

   b. Record what God is teaching you in your worship journal.

4. In this chapter you read three stories of surrender: Lorraine's, Dr. Wilson's, and F. B. Meyer's. Which story could you most identify with? Write a paragraph explaining why you chose the story you did.

5. Paraphrase Romans 11:33-12:2. Write it in such a simple way that a child could understand it.

6. Read the prayer of surrender on page 99. Find some time this week (at least thirty minutes) to be quiet before the Lord. Ask Him to give you wisdom as you fill out the lists below.

All that I am   All that I have

All that I do   All that I suffer

7. Read John 14:21,23-24; 15:10. From these verses, write your own thoughts of how love and obedience flow together.

8. Express in a creative way what the promises found in Psalm 25:14 and John 14:21 say to you: Write a poem or a song, draw a picture, make a collage, or write a letter to a friend sharing the joy of these promises. (Use your imagination.)

Now, take out your journal and record your answers to these questions.

9. What did you learn about God this week?

10. What did you learn about worship this week?

11. What did you learn about yourself this week?

WEEK 6

I Bow My Words

1. Read chapter 6, "I Bow My Words," two times.

2. This week you get to choose the verses to memorize. Select two from the following verses: Proverbs 12:18; Proverbs 18:21; James 3:9-10; and Ephesians 4:29-30. Write your verses here and use them in your times of worship and prayer this week.

3. Read 1 Thessalonians 5:11 and Hebrews 10:24-25. Each day this week covet before God to say one word of encouragement to your husband and children. If you are single, commit to encourage your roommate, a coworker, or a friend every day this week. Write a summary of what you learned through doing this exercise.

4. Practice the Twenty-Minute Worship Experience. Spend ten to twenty minutes a day in private worship. Suggestions for this time:

   a. Read aloud and personalize in prayer Psalm 66 and Psalm 71.

   b. Kneel or sit in silence before God for ten minutes asking Him to let you hear His voice.

5. Read Proverbs 12:18 and 18:21. Rewrite these two verses using word pictures. Write them so simply that a child could understand them.

6. Read James 3:1-12.

   a. Have an honest talk with God about your words. Tell Him how these verses make you feel.

   b. Make a list of positive statements (at least five) that you can use to bless God and others.

7. Read Ephesians 4:29-30.

   a. What is your sin pattern when it comes to your words?
      Sarcasm? Criticism? Negativism? Lying? Too many
      words? Or something else? Name your sin pattern
      here.

   b. Write a prayer to God, asking for His power in this
      area and detailing how you plan to work toward
      change.

8. Amy Carmichael asked these three questions to help keep
   from sinning with her words:

   Is it kind? Is it true? Is it necessary?

   How could these questions help you worship God with your
   words? How would viewing your words as an act of worship
   encourage you in your area of weakness?

9. There is an intimate link, both negative and positive,
   between the Holy Spirit and our words. Read Ephesians
   4:29-30 and 5:18-19.

a. Tell about a time when you grieved the Spirit with your words.

b. Describe a situation in which you lived out Ephesians 5:18-19.

c. Describe how Ephesians 5:18-19 can become a lifestyle for you.

Now, take out your journal and record your answers to these questions.

10. What did you learn about God this week?

11. What did you learn about worship this week?

12. What did you learn about yourself this week?

WEEK 7

I Bow My Attitude

1. Read chapter 7, "I Bow My Attitude," two times.

2. Memorize Hebrews 13:15 and Colossians 2:7. Write the verses here.

3. Practice the Twenty-Minute Worship Experience. Spend ten to twenty minutes each day in worship. Suggestions for your time:

   a. Prayerfully read Revelation 21.

   b. Read Psalm 50 and meditate on it as you worship.

4. Read the definition of the word *attitude* and the quote from Chuck Swindoll on page 128.

   a. What helps you to move your will and take sides with an attitude of gratitude? List at least three things.

   b. Explain why you agree or disagree with Chuck
      Swindoll's quote.

5. Read Exodus 14 — 17:7.

   a. What do you learn about gratitude from the Israelites?

   b. What do you learn about grumbling?

   c. What is God's message to you in these chapters?

6. Read Luke 17:11-19.

   a. Relate a time when you acted like the nine "forgetful
      lepers."

   b. What will help you to remember to thank God?

   c. Select two projects to do from the "Come, Let's Get Practical" section on pages 138-141. Write down what you learned from doing these projects.

7. Make a conscious effort to listen to yourself this week. Ask God to make you aware of your attitude. Fill out this chart each day, rating yourself from 1-10 (10 being most gracious) on your attitude.

	Gratitude	Grumbling
Monday		
Tuesday		
Wednesday		
Thursday		
Friday		
Saturday		
Sunday		

8. Read Hebrews 13:15-16. Write a paragraph describing what the two kinds of sacrifices mentioned in these verses look like in your life.

9. Read Ephesians 5:20. What does it look like for you to give thanks in ALL things?

Now, take out your journal and record your answers to these questions.

10. What did you learn about God this week?

11. What did you learn about worship this week?

12. What did you learn about yourself this week?

13. Write a prayer to God expressing how you desire to worship Him with your attitude.

WEEK 8

I Bow My Work

1. Read chapter 8, "I Bow My Work," two times.

2. Memorize and meditate on Colossians 3:23-24.

    a. Write the verses here.

    b. Write a paragraph, personalizing Colossians 3:23-24.

3. Practice the Twenty-Minute Worship Experience. Spend ten to twenty minutes a day in private worship. Here are some suggestions for the time:

    a. Ask God to teach you about worship.

    b. Meditate on Psalm 90; Psalm 5; and Psalm 16.

4. Read Matthew 25:14-30. The talents represent a sum of money but can also be looked at as opportunities.

a. How were the talents distributed, and what implications does this have for you?

b. What was the basis on which servants were rewarded? Compare this with 1 Corinthians 4:2.

5. List the categories of work you do at this stage of life. (Categories might be office work, housework, "Mom work," church work, and so on.) Then list the two or three main things you do in each category.

6. What were the messages you received as a child about success?

a. How do these messages match up with the truth of God's Word?

b. Read Colossians 3:23-24 again. How do these verses
    define success for you?

7. Look at the list of reasons why some women feel their
    work is insignificant on page 151. Which three do you most
    identify with and why?

8. Do you consider some work more sacred than other work?
    Be honest and explain your answer.

a. What is God's view of creative gifts as revealed in
    Exodus 35:25-33?

b. How does this passage encourage you concerning your
    work?

9. Write here the meaning of the Latin words *Laborare est Orare. Orare est Laborare.*

    a. How would you describe *Laborare est Orare. Orare est Laborare.* to a friend who is grumbling about her work?

    b. Make a plaque with the Latin words for your place of work.

    c. How can you apply these words this week to the areas of your work that you listed under question 5?

Now, take out your journal and record your answers to these questions.

10. What did you learn about God this week?

11. What did you learn about worship this week?

12. What did you learn about yourself this week?

WEEK 9

I Bow My Times of Waiting

1. Read chapter 9, "I Bow My Times of Waiting," two times.

2. Memorize and meditate on Psalm 31:14-15. Write the verses here.

3. Practice the Twenty-Minute Worship Experience. Spend ten to twenty minutes a day in private worship. Suggestions for this time: Pray through Psalm 31 and Psalm 18. Meditate on these beautiful psalms of David.

4. Are you in "waiting mode" now? What are you waiting for God to answer?

5. Read Psalm 27:13-14; Psalm 25:5; and Psalm 31:14-15.

    a. Describe a time that you, like David, trusted God with your time of waiting.

b. Read Matthew 16:15-23.

c. Describe a time you acted like Peter and got in God's way.

6. The three reasons we get in God's way are:

   1. We only know part of the story.

   2. We are prompted to "fix a problem" because we care.

   3. We are prompted to "fix" in order to protect ourselves.

   Which of these three do you most identify with? Why?

7. Paraphrase Psalm 27. How do these words of David encourage you?

8. Read the four practical suggestions on pages 172-178: *Ask, Stand, Rock,* and *Fly.*

Choose two of these to apply to your "waiting" situation and explain how you will do this.

9. Read the poem "Waiting" on pages 179-180, and then journal your thoughts and feelings.

10. Write a prayer to God expressing how you want to bow your timeline to Him and say, "My times are in your hands."

Now, take out your journal and record your answers to these questions.

11. What did you learn about God this week?

12. What did you learn about worship this week?

13. What did you learn about yourself this week?

WEEK 10

I Bow My Pain

1. Read chapter 10, "I Bow My Pain," two times.

2. Memorize 2 Corinthians 4:8-9. Write the verses here.

3. Practice the Twenty-Minute Worship Experience. Spend ten to twenty minutes a day in private worship. Suggestions for your time:

   a. Meditate and personalize Psalm 20.

   b. Read aloud and pray Psalm 142 to God.

   c. Read Psalm 27 and pray it personally to God.

4. According to 2 Corinthians 1:3-4, Paul experienced God's comfort.

   a. Read 2 Corinthians 1:3-4.

   b. Paraphrase these verses.

c. Give two examples of how God has comforted you.

d. Has God used you to comfort someone with the "ministry of comfort"? Describe what that looked like.

5. According to 2 Corinthians 1:8-9, Paul exchanged self-confidence for God-confidence.

a. Read 2 Corinthians 1:8-9.

b. Paraphrase these verses.

c. List several ways that God has changed you through painful times.

d. What does it look like for you to move from self-confidence to God-confidence?

6. According to 2 Corinthians 4:8-9, Paul learned to live on the side of triumph.

   a. Read 2 Corinthians 4:8-9.

   b. Write these verses so a child could understand them.

   c. Look at the listings under The Side of Agony/The Side of Triumph on pages 191-197: (hard pressed BUT NOT crushed, perplexed BUT NOT in despair, persecuted BUT NOT abandoned, and struck down BUT NOT destroyed). Choose two that you have experienced. Describe how you have been able to move from the side of agony to the side of triumph.

7. You met Valerie in chapters 9 and 10. Use descriptive words to share how her supernatural healing makes you feel. How has God provided a way of escape for you during a painful time?

8. According to 2 Corinthians 2:14-15, Paul's pain became a fragrant offering.

   a. Read 2 Corinthians 2:14-15.

   b. Read the story on pages 198-199 about the carrot, egg, and coffee bean. Which are you? Explain your answer.

9. Which of the four suggestions under the "Come, Let's Get Practical" section have you tried? Express how you could apply the others.

Now, take out your journal and record your answers to these questions.

10. What did you learn about God this week?

11. What did you learn about worship this week?

12. What did you learn about yourself this week?

WEEK 11

I Bow My Will

1. Read chapter 11, "I Bow My Will," two times.

2. Choose two of these verses to memorize and meditate on: Matthew 26:39; Genesis 22:14; Job 1:21; and Habakkuk 3:18-19. Write the verses here.

3. Practice the Twenty-Minute Worship Experience. Spend ten to twenty minutes a day in private worship. Suggestions for your time:

    a. Worship God with the ABCs of Worship. (To refresh your memory, refer to the end of chapter 2.)

    b. Worship God with all the names of God the Father, God the Son, and God the Spirit that you can bring to mind.

    c. Worship God with Psalm 91; Psalm 40; and Psalm 84.

4. Read Matthew 26:31-46.

    a. Why do you think Jesus prayed, "Thy will be done" three times?

b. Describe a time when you agonized in prayer to bow your will.

5. Read Job 1.

a. List all the things you learn about Job in this chapter.

b. How was Job able to live verses 20-22? What message is there in these verses for you?

6. Read Habakkuk 3:16-19.

a. What do you learn from Habakkuk about bowing your will to God's will?

7. Answer the next few questions when you can have a half hour of uninterrupted time alone.

a. Read the story of the Isaac altar in Genesis 22:1-18. Ask God to give you deep understanding as you read.

b. What do you think Abraham learned about God through this experience?

c. What did God learn about Abraham?

8. What is your Isaac? Name it and write it down on a piece of paper.

a. Bow in worship and still your heart before Him. Tell Him you have come to build your altar with tears and trembling hands.

b. How do you lay your Isaac on the altar? You can:

❧ Pray a prayer like this: My Father, right now I give _____ to you. He is yours. I trust him to you. I lift _____ and bind him with the hands of my heart to the Isaac altar. I bow my will to your will. Receive it, precious Lord, as my worship.

❧ Act out your relinquishment by literally lifting _____ to the altar and binding him to the wood.

9. Spend some time worshipping your great God. Write a prayer thanking Him for giving you the strength and courage to bow your will to His will.

Now, take out your journal and record your answers to these questions.

10. What did you learn about God this week?

11. What did you learn about worship this week?

12. What did you learn about yourself this week?

WEEK 12

Drawn into His Presence

1. Read chapter 12, "Drawn into His Presence," two times.

2. Memorize Psalm 63:1-2. Write it here.

3. Practice the Twenty-Minute Worship Experience. Spend ten to twenty minutes a day in private worship. During this time you could meditate on or read aloud:

   Psalm 16: Psalm 89; or Psalm 42.

4. Write your definition of *worship*.

   a. Look back at week 1, question 13 in the study and compare the definition of worship you wrote then with what you wrote above.

b. How has your view of worship expanded in these twelve weeks?

5. Look up the following verses. What aspect of God's presence is described in each one?

Isaiah 9:3

Acts 3:19

Psalm 46:10

Acts 2:28

Exodus 33:14

Psalm 16:11

Psalm 42:5

6. Look back through the first eleven weeks of this study. (You can also refer to the summaries of each chapter on pages 227-229.)

a. Write a letter to a friend describing what God has taught you about worship.

b. Spend time thanking God for what you have learned and how you have grown as a worshipper.

7. Describe what it looks like for you to have scheduled appointments with God.

a. Who initiates these times of meeting — you or God?

b. What scheduled appointments have you had this week with God?

8. Read the surprise encounters on pages 233-236.

a. List at least three things you learned about God through reading these encounters.

b. Who initiates surprise encounters — you or God?

c. Have you ever experienced a surprise encounter with God?

d. If you feel comfortable, describe the encounter and express why you think God came to you as He did.

9. Which of the three men — Brother Lawrence, Frank Laubach, or Thomas Kelly — did you most identify with? Write a paragraph explaining your answer and what you learned from him.

Now, take out your journal and record your answers to these questions.

10. What did you learn about God in this twelve-week Bible study?

11. What did you learn about worship in this twelve-week Bible study?

12. What did you learn about yourself in this twelve-week Bible study?

Notes

Chapter 1: My Thirsty Soul

1. Bob Sorge, *Secrets of the Secret Place* (Lee's Summit, MO: Oasis House, 2001), 179-180.
2. J. Oswald Sanders, *Enjoying Intimacy with God* (Chicago, IL: Moody, 1980), 14.
3. John F. Walvoord and Roy B. Zuck, *The Bible Knowledge Commentary,* Vol. 2 (Wheaton, IL: Victor, 1983), 661.
4. Sam Storms, *Pleasures Evermore* (Colorado Springs, CO: NavPress, 2000), 54.
5. John Piper, *The Pleasures of God: Meditations on God's Delight in Being God* (Portland, OR: Multnomah, 1991), 17.
6. C. S. Lewis, quoted by Joseph Carroll, *How to Worship Jesus Christ* (Chicago IL:Moody, 1997), 12.
7. Storms, 42.

Chapter 2: My Worship Awakening

1. A. W. Tozer, *Whatever Happened to Worship?* (Camp Hill, PA: Christian Publications, 1985), 86.
2. Ronald Allen and Gordon Borror, *Worship: Rediscovering the Missing Jewel* (Portland, OR: Multnomah, 1982), 16.
3. Watchman Nee, *Worship God* (New York: Christian Fellowship, 1990), 36.
4. A. W. Tozer, *The Tozer Topical Reader*, Vol. Two, complied by Ron Eggert (Camp Hill, PA: Christian Publications, 1998), 281.
5. Victor Hugo, *Les Misérables*, chapter 1.
6. Joseph Carroll, *How to Worship Jesus Christ* (Chicago, IL: Moody, 1997), 15.
7. Carroll, 15.
8. A. P. Gibbs, *Worship* (Denver: Wilson Foundation, nd), 26.
9. Tozer, *Whatever Happened to Worship?*, 88.
10. W. E. Vine and F. F. Bruce, *Vine's Expository Dictionary of Old and New Testament Words*, Vol. II (Old Tappan, NJ: Revell, 1981), 235.

11. George Skramstad, quoted in *Renovare Perspective*, Vol. 7, No. 4.

12. LaMar Boschman, *A Heart of Worship* (Orlando, FL: Creation House, 1994), 7.

CHAPTER 3: MY SOUL FINDS STILLNESS

1. LaMar Boschman, *A Heart of Worship* (Orlando, FL: Creation House, 1994), 23.

2. Thomas Merton, quoted by Ronald Rolheiser, *The Shattered Lantern* (London, England: Hodder and Stoughton, 1994), 34.

3. Henri Nouwen, *Making All Things New: An Introduction to the Spiritual Life* (New York: Doubleday, 1981), 23.

4. Martha Kilpatrick, *Adoration* (Sargent, GA: SeedSowers, 1999), 19.

5. Kilpatrick, 107.

6. Mrs. Charles E. Cowman, *Streams in the Desert* (Grand Rapids, MI: Zondervan, 1925), June 13, 189.

7. Rolheiser, 36.

8. O. Hallesby, *Under His Wings* (Minneapolis, MN: Augsburg, 1932), 13.

9. Richard J. Foster, *Celebration of Discipline* (San Francisco, CA: Harper-Collins, 1978), 105-106.

10. Richard J. Foster, *Prayers from the Heart* (London, England: Hodder and Stoughton, 1996), 59.

CHAPTER 4: EXPANDING MY WORSHIP EXPERIENCE

1. Andrew Murray, *With Christ in the School of Prayer* (Westwood, NJ: Fleming H. Revell, 1967), 28.

2. John MacArthur Jr., *The Ultimate Priority: On Worship* (Chicago: Moody, 1983), 115-116.

3. Gerrit Gustafson, *Be a Better Worshiper! Study Guide* (Brentwood, TN: Worship Schools, 2004), 15.

4. Marcos Witt, *A Worship-Filled Life* (Orlando, FL: Creation House, 1998), 66.

5. MacArthur, 116-117.

6. Watchman Nee, *Worship God* (New York: Christian Fellowship, 1990), 20-21.

7. Adapted from an email from Dr. Sam Storms, Enjoying God Ministries, Monday, October 10, 2005.
8. Hannah Hurnard, *Winged Life* (Wheaton, IL: Tyndale, 1978), 85.

Chapter 5: I Bow My Life

1. V. Raymond Edman, *They Found the Secret* (Grand Rapids, MI: Zondervan, 1960), 153-154.
2. Edman, 154-155.
3. Adapted from Joseph Carroll, *How to Worship Jesus Christ* (Chicago: Moody, 1997), 26.
4. Ney Bailey heard this prayer given by Elisabeth Elliot. She does not recall the date or place of this message.
5. Lawrence O. Richard, *Expository Dictionary of Bible Words* (Grand Rapids, MI: Zondervan, 1985), 462.
6. A. W. Tozer, *The Tozer Topical Reader,* Vol. One, compiled by Ron Eggert (Camp Hill, PA: Christian Publications, 1998), 324.
7. W. E. Vine, *An Expository Dictionary of New Testament Words* (Nashville, TN: Thomas Nelson, 1952), 795.

Chapter 6: I Bow My Words

1. Charles R. Swindoll, *Growing Strong in the Seasons of Life* (Portland, OR: Multnomah, 1983), 28.
2. Paul Lee Tan, *Encyclopedia of 7700 Illustrations* (Rockville, MD: Assurance Publishers, 1979), 1421.
3. R.V.G. Tasker, *The General Epistle of James* (London, England: The Tyndale Press, 1957), 78.
4. Robert Johnstone, *Lectures on the Epistle of James* (Minneapolis, MN: Klock and Klock, 1871), 264.
5. Tan, 1423.
6. Lawrence J. Crabb Jr. and Dan B. Allender, *Encouragement: The Key to Caring* (Grand Rapids, MI: Zondervan, 1984), 24-25.
7. William Arndt, Frederick W. Danker, and Walter Bauer, *A Greek-English Lexicon of the New Testament and Other Early Christian Literature*, 3rd ed. (Chicago: University of Chicago Press, 2000), 766.

8. Elisabeth Elliot, *A Chance to Die* (Grand Rapids, MI: Revell, 2005).
9. Tan, 3648, 848.

CHAPTER 7: I BOW MY ATTITUDE

1. Robert Jeffress, *Choose Your Attitudes, Change Your Life* (Wheaton, IL: Victor, 1992), 11.
2. Jeffress, 18.
3. Colin Brown, editor, *Dictionary of New Testament Theology*, Vol. 2 (Grand Rapids, MI: Zondervan, 1976), 616.
4. Brown, 617.
5. Charles R. Swindoll, *Strengthening Your Grip* (Waco, TX: Word, 1982), 206-207.
6. Marcos Witt, *A Worship-Filled Life* (Orlando, FL: Creation House, 1998), 2.
7. "Murphy's Law" (231 Adrian Road, Millbrae, CA, Celestial Arts, 1979).
8. Jerry Bridges, *The Practice of Godliness* (Colorado Springs, CO: NavPress, 1983), 101-102.
9. Michael P. Green, *Illustrations for Biblical Preaching* (Grand Rapids, MI: Baker, 1982), 376.
10. Green, 376-377.
11. This quote was passed around on the Internet. I have not been able to find an author.

CHAPTER 8: I BOW MY WORK

1. The phrase, *Laborare est orare. Orare est laborare* when translated word for word from Latin, means "To work is to pray. To pray is to work." However, pastor and writer Stuart Brisco and the poem at the end of the chapter by Thomas Hanford translate the phrase as "To work is to worship. To worship is to work." The *Latin to English Dictionary* says both "pray" and "worship" are English possibilities of the Latin word *orare*.
2. Stuart Briscoe, *Choices for a Lifetime* (Wheaton, IL: Tyndale, 1995), 135.
3. Jamie Winship, "Labor of Love," *Discipleship Journal*, Jan/Feb 2000, 39.
4. Sue Kline, "Sacred Work," *Discipleship Journal*, Jan/Feb 2000, 10.

5. Tom Kraeuter, Worship Is WHAT?! (Lynnwood, WA: Emerald Books, 1996, 1996), 84.
6. A. W. Tozer, *Gems from Tozer* (Send the Light Trust, 1969), 7.
7. Thomas W. Hanford, *Two Thousand and Ten Choice Quotations in Poetry and Prose* (n.p. 1985), 32.
8. I found this quote on the Internet and have been unable to identify the author.

CHAPTER 9: I BOW MY TIMES OF WAITING

1. Andrew Murray, *Waiting on God* (New Kensington, PA: Whitaker House, 1981), 39-40.
2. F. Brown, S. R. Driver, and C. A. Briggs, *Enhanced Brown-Driver-Briggs Hebrew and English Lexicon* Strong's, TWOT, and GK references (Oak Harbor, WA: Logos Research Systems, 2000), electronic ed., xiii.
3. Bob Sorge, *In His Face* (Greenwood, MO: Oasis, 1994), 24.
4. Murray, 91.
5. I found this poem on the Internet and have been unable to identify the author.

CHAPTER 10: I BOW MY PAIN

1. Hannah Hurnard, *Hinds' Feet on High Places* (Wheaton, IL: Tyndale, 1975), 82.
2. Alan Redpath, *Blessings out of Buffetings, Studies in Second Corinthians* (Old Tappan, NJ: Fleming H. Revell, 1965), 12.
3. Redpath, 12.
4. Redpath, 16.
5. J. P. Lange, D. D., and the Rev. F. R. Fay, *Langes Commentary on the Holy Scriptures* Vol. 10, Romans and Corinthians (Grand Rapids, MI: Zondervan, 1960), 75.
6. Oswald Chambers, *My Utmost for His Highest* (Uhrichsville, OH: Barbour, 1935), May 19th.
7. Lange, 75.
8. I received this story in an email. I have not been able to find the source.
9. Jack R. Taylor, *The Hallelujah Factor* (Nashville, TN: Broadman, 1983), 30-31.

10. Ron Mehl, *The Cure for a Troubled Heart* (Sisters, OR: Multnomah, 1996), 46.

CHAPTER 11: I BOW MY WILL

1. Charles Spurgeon, *The Joy in Praising God* (New Kensington, PA: Whitaker House, 1995), 19.
2. James Swanson, *Dictionary of Biblical Languages with Semantic Domains:* Hebrew (Old Testament), electronic ed., DBLH 1635 (Oak Harbor, WA: Logos Research Systems).
3. Alred Edersheim, *Sketches of Jewish Social Life in the Days of Christ* (Grand Rapids, MI: Eerdmans, 1967), 104.
4. Lysa TerKeurst, *Radically Obedient, Radically Blessed* (Eugene, OR: Harvest House, 2003), 37.
5. *Webster's New World Dictionary of the American Language, s.v.* "Relinquish," 841.
6. Carol Kent, *When I Lay My Isaac Down* (Colorado Springs, CO: NavPress, 2004), 53.
7. Kent, 43.
8. This list is adapted from Joseph Carroll, *How to Worship Jesus Christ* (Chicago: Moody, 1997), 21.

CHAPTER 12: DRAWN INTO HIS PRESENCE

1. Peter Rowe, *The Presence of God* (Kent, England: Sovereign World Limited, 1996), 15.
2. Rowe, 15.
3. Brenda J. Davis, *"Dancing with your Husband,"* SpiritLed Women, February/March 2007, 7.
4. Adapted from Pat Chen, *Intimacy with the Beloved* (Lake Mary, FL.: Creation House, 2000), 1-5.
5. James W. Goll, *The Lost Art of Practicing His Presence* (Shippensburg, PA: Destiny Image, 2005), 230-231.
6. Brother Lawrence, *The Practice of the Presence of God* (Grand Rapids, MI: Fleming H. Revell, 1958), 77-78.
7. Brother Lawrence and Frank Laubach, *Practicing His Presence* (Sargent, GA: The SeedSowers, first printed 1692), 102.
8. Lawrence and Laubach, 106.
9. Lawrence and Laubach, 13-14.
10. Lawrence and Laubach, 10.

11. Lawrence and Laubach, 22.
12. Lawrence and Laubach, 22-23.
13. Thomas R. Kelly, *A Testament of Devotion* (San Francisco, CA: Harper, 1941), 9.

About the Author

LINDA DILLOW and her husband, Jody, have lived in Europe and Asia and have been involved in international ministry for twenty-five years. Linda speaks at women's retreats and conferences in America, Asia, and Europe.

Her books include *Calm My Anxious Heart*, *A Deeper Kind of Calm*, and *Creative Counterpart*, as well as *Intimate Issues* and *Intimacy Ignited*, coauthored with Lorraine Pintus.

She and her husband now live in Monument, Colorado. They have four grown children and are grandparents.

MORE GREAT BOOKS FROM BEST-SELLING AUTHOR LINDA DILLOW.

My Worship Journey
ISBN-13: 978-1-57683-391-9

The companion journal to *Satisfy My Thirsty Soul* will help you establish your own lifestyle of worship.

Calm My Anxious Heart
ISBN-13: 978-1-60006-141-7

Women worry a lot. We worry about our children, our friends, our careers, our families, our spouses — the list could go on and on. With *Calm My Anxious Heart* you can let go of your anxiety and experience the contentment that comes from trusting God.

My Journey to Contentment
ISBN-13: 978-1-60006-186-8

The companion journal to *Calm My Anxious Heart* will help you focus on growing in contentment and faith as you learn to trust God completely.